D1414827

Parenting
One Day
at a Time

Parenting One Day at a Time

*Using the Tools of Recovery
to Become Better Parents
and Raise Better Kids*

ALEX J. PACKER, PH.D.

50th
1949-1999
HAZELDEN

HAZELDEN®

INFORMATION & EDUCATIONAL SERVICES

Hazelden
Center City, Minnesota 55012-0176

1-800-328-0094
1-651-213-4590 (Fax)
www.hazelden.org

Library of Congress Cataloging-in-Publication Data
Packer, Alex J., date.
    Parenting one day at a time: using the tools of recovery to become better
    parents and raise better kids / Alex J. Packer.
        p.   cm.
    Originally published: New York: Dell Trade Paperback, c1996.
    Includes bibliographical references and index.
    ISBN 1-56838-323-1
    1. Recovering alcoholics—Family relationships.   2. Recovering
    addicts—Family relationships.   3. Children of alcoholics.
    4. Children of narcotic addicts.   5. Parent and child.
    6. Parenting.   I. Title.
    [HV5132.P33 1999]
    362.292'4—dc21   98-48414
                                                                    CIP

Editor's note
All the stories in this book are based on actual experiences. The names and
details have been changed to protect the privacy of the people involved. In
some cases, composites have been created.

03 02 01 00 99 6 5 4 3 2 1

Cover design by Theresa Gedig
Interior design by Donna Burch
Typesetting by Stanton Publication Services, Inc.

to Jack Winter-Rose

Contents

Acknowledgments

I would like to thank the following individuals and institutions for their advice, support, and expertise. Without them, the researching and writing of this book would not have been possible.

Randy Ingham, Nate Keedy, Cindy Lanane, Phil McCartin, Joy Natoli, and Bill Scalise at the Family Counseling and Guidance Centers of Massachusetts; Peg Coogan at St. Elizabeth's Hospital in Boston; Marion Oxenhorn and Matt Cornish at Hi Point in Plymouth and Tewksbury, Massachusetts; The Hazelden Foundation.

Lou Argow, Karen Cassidy, Michael Clarke, Paula Donius, Bill Gregory, Stephen Gustin, Ross Herbertson, Norman Jenkins, Leroy Kelly, Suzanne Laberge, Milly Leedy, Murray Mahool, Powers McLeod, Jack Peckham, Pat Smith, Kate Yamokoski.

Maureen McGlame, senior clinician, Massachusetts General Hospital; founder, COASA (Children of Alcoholism and Substance Abuse, Inc.).

Ann Donaruma, Eugene Gonzales, Drs. John Dacey, Maureen Kenny, and John Travers at Boston College.

My agents, Gail Ross and Howard Yoon, of Lichtman, Trister, Singer & Ross.

Caryn Pernu, Free Spirit Publishing, Inc.

The many members of Twelve Step recovery programs who shared their experience, strength, and hope so that it might benefit other parents in recovery.

And finally, Donald F. Cutler Jr. and the staff and teachers at FCD Educational Services, Inc., Needham, Massachusetts, for

their tireless work in schools across the United States and abroad
to

- provide up-to-date information on the physiological
  and psychological effects of alcohol and other drugs;
- promote awareness of chemical dependency as a
  primary, progressive, and often fatal disease;
- empower young people to make healthy, responsible
  choices regarding alcohol and other drug use;
- encourage and support the non-use of alcohol and
  other drugs during the growing years.

Part One

First Things First

1

How It Works

. . . Remember that we deal with children—cunning, baffling, powerful! Without help it is too much for us.[1]

This book applies the principles of Twelve Step programs to the challenge of raising children. It shows parents how to use the tools and wisdom of recovery to become better parents and raise better kids.

The premise for this book rests on three simple ideas:

1. Children raised by dependent parents internalize and act out many of the feelings, attitudes, and behaviors of the dependent parent.

2. In recovery we learn a new manner of living that allows us to grow along spiritual lines and replace negative character traits with positive ones.

3. The tools that inspire our personal growth can inspire our growth as parents and the growth of our children—with the same miraculous results!

We discover in recovery that living one day at a time restores our sanity and revitalizes our spirit. Living one day at a time brings balance, perspective, and joy into our lives. This is not to say that we ignore the past or neglect the future. Rather, we recognize that the best way to prepare for tomorrow is to focus on the quality of today. This philosophy lies at the heart of *one-day-at-a-time* parenting.

One-day-at-a-time parents ask

- What does my child need from me now?
- What can I do today to improve the quality of my relationship with my child?
- What can I do today to strengthen my child's emotional and spiritual health?

One-day-at-a-time parents *keep it simple.* A recovering father of two teenagers explained what this meant in his family: "As my wife doesn't eat meat, and my daughter doesn't eat tomatoes, and my son doesn't eat beans, I no longer use four separate pots to cook my chili. We just don't eat chili."

One-day-at-a-time parents seek *progress not perfection.* Said a single mother with two years of sobriety: "I recognize that my kids are never static. They are always progressing *somewhere,* although I now see that it's not necessarily in a linear manner to destinations that exist in the great order of things worked out by me."

One-day-at-a-time parents practice *humility.* Said a mother in early recovery: "I'm learning to ask my kids what *they* think instead of telling them how it is."

One recovering father noted a more egalitarian approach to limit setting: "Rules evolve from experience now that I no longer receive them on tablets from Mount Blackout. When we have a conflict, we try to follow our 'group conscience.'"

The conceptual foundations of recovery—patience, acceptance, honesty, gratitude, faith, humility, responsibility—are powerful, *proven* tools for personal growth. But does this approach really work with kids? Can we take what is intended as a personal program of recovery and apply it to child raising? Absolutely.

Recovery *is* child raising. In recovery we learn how to take care of ourselves, how to solve problems and deal with conflict, how to respect the needs and feelings of others, how to behave morally and responsibly, how to build trusting, intimate relationships. We learn values and perspective, honesty and compassion, generosity and forgiveness. We learn about our place in society and our place in the universe. We learn to accept ourselves while we strive to improve ourselves. Isn't this what child raising is all about? Aren't these the very things we wish to teach our children?

At this point you may think: *Dream on. I'm having enough trouble learning these things myself. How am I going to teach them to anyone else?* You may look at your family relationships and the needs of your children and feel hopeless, inadequate: *It's too late. I'll never be a good parent.*

Nonsense! You will become a good parent.

Why am I so confident of your chances for success? Three reasons:

1. You already know the language. You "speak" it every day. You know what it means to *keep it simple,* to *turn it over,* to *live and let live.* You have experienced the curative power of acceptance, trust, faith, and friendship.

2. You already understand your children far better than you know. Earlier I mentioned that the children of alcoholics and other drug addicts internalize their parents' attitudes and behaviors. (This may be one reason why so many of them grow up to become, or to marry, substance abusers.) These children feel powerless, ashamed, guilty, resentful, and scared. They are often impulsive, disorganized, and hypercritical of themselves and others. They tend to feel abnormal and anxious, to lie and shrink from criticism, to dread making mistakes. They are usually compulsively responsible—or irresponsible.

   They are—in so many ways—just like you. At times they may seem like strangers, but they are not. You know them. You know what it's like to feel unworthy and unwelcome, lonely and inadequate. Of course, because they are children, and because they were thrust into a home and a situation over which they had no control, they feel and see things differently too. But the commonality of your experience can be used to nourish the acceptance and empathy that are key to family healing.

3. The third reason I am confident you will be able to use the tools of recovery to become a better parent is because this book is going to show you how. It is a practical book. It teaches concrete skills you can use to resolve conflict, build trust, and communicate honestly and respectfully. It takes concepts you're already using or learning—making amends, asking for help, letting go, living in today—and demonstrates how they apply to the everyday issues all parents face. It explains why an approach to child raising based on the tools and slogans of recovery is the *best* approach to child raising—not just for parents in recovery, but for all parents.

A Few Notes on Language

I will use the terms *alcoholics* and *addicts* interchangeably as my primary means of referring to *all* individuals with chemical and/or behavioral addictions. I recognize that many of the readers of this book will not be alcoholics and that many alcoholics may not consider themselves addicts. We learn in recovery, however, that the emotions, attitudes, and character traits associated with addiction transcend any one drug or behavior. Therefore, I ask you to transcend the specific words I use. When I speak of alcoholism or addiction, I am speaking of any and all dependencies—be they to food, drugs, behaviors, or relationships.

I have adopted the first person plural—*we*—as the "speaking" voice for this book. This is not the royal *we* (although I would be less than honest if I didn't admit to certain pretensions in that direction). Rather, this is the "we're-all-in-this-together" *we*.

In the past we obsessed on our uniqueness, on how we were different from everyone else. In so doing we felt isolated and alone. We made ourselves miserable. In recovery, we discover how much we have in common with others. It is this sharing, this connectedness, this "*us*-ness" that I wish to stress.

There's just one problem, though. When I write "we addicts" and "those of us who were sexually abused as children" and "our alcoholic fathers who hit us," I picture my own parents reading this book and having two fits apiece: "What do you mean by saying that? We never abused you! We're not alcoholics. Everyone is going to think you're talking about us!" Therefore, let me hasten to add that I use the first person plural voice as a linguistic convenience. It is not meant to suggest that the thoughts, feelings, behaviors, abuses, addictions, childhood experiences, and/or parenting practices I ascribe to "us" apply to me, in part or in totality, any more than they do to you.

2

The Promises

Now that we are in recovery, we have come face-to-face with the need to repair our families and to learn again, or for the first time, the skills of healthy child raising. We realize that recovery must extend to our children, our relationships, and our attitudes and behaviors as parents.

So, do we face this challenge with optimism and courage? Do we feel confident that the tools we use to heal ourselves can be used to heal our children? Do we heed the miracle of our own recovery to believe in a new one for our family?

Nah!

Well, perhaps a few of us do—if we have been clean and sober for a while or have stockpiled enough faith and self-confidence to face life with courage and hope. We may even be that rare bird, the *Alcoholic Positivus* (I think two have been sighted in North America this century), distinguished by its exuberant, can-do attitude: *Of course I can become a better parent if I try; of course I can help my family to heal.*

Most of us card-carrying addicts, however, tend to follow a different credo:

- Approach all new challenges with trepidation.
- Identify pitfalls early and remain focused on the negative.

- Begin every sentence with *but.*
- Turn down all offers of help.
- If one doubt will do, always take two.

Sound familiar? It should, for these tendencies constitute the Alcoholic at Rest. They are normal and natural—and we must fight them every step of the way.

When we first came into recovery, we carried so much baggage, it's a wonder we fit through the door. We were lost, angry, vulnerable, and out of control. Some of us made an instant connection—love at first sight. Others of us came kicking and screaming. We sat in meetings terrified that we would be called on to speak, and we were indignant when we were not. We were so busy rehearsing our own words, we heard few of anyone else's. We mouthed slogans and pasted on gratitude. We took everyone's inventory but our own. We longed for connection, yet raced off at the end of each meeting lest we might make one. We decided we had nothing in common with these "grateful" alcoholics who glowed with serenity, who had the arrogance to be humble, who spoke of God as if He were their next-door neighbor. And, if we needed any more proof that we were surrounded by a bunch of lunatics, these people actually accepted us! How could we possibly respect them after that? We mistrusted these Serene Ones. They were everything we wanted to be.

What kept us going? The Promises. Promises we didn't believe—but didn't dare not believe. Promises of a new freedom and a new happiness, of serenity and peace. We were told that we would lose our fear and self-pity. We would come to accept the past. We would grow spiritually. Self-seeking would slip away, and in its place would come a new interest in others. "It gets better," they said.

So we kept coming back, hoping to find the "promised" land. And if today we have not yet found peace and serenity, we know that we have come, one step at a time, that much closer. We have tasted a new freedom and a new happiness. Our worst days now are better than our best days then.

Our efforts to become better parents, like our efforts to stay clean and sober, are going to be stalked by old character defects: fear, guilt, self-pity, self-doubt, self-seeking. Old voices will work overtime to drown out the new. Our faith will be challenged. There will be times when we'll feel like giving up. We mustn't. We *will* become good parents. We *will* bring healing to our families. We *will* build better relationships with our children. But in order to do so, we need to believe in a new set of promises.

The Parent's Promises

If we apply the tools of recovery to the tasks of child raising, we will be amazed at the results. We will know a new freedom from worry, guilt, and conflict. We will know a new happiness as we witness the growth of our children into moral, caring beings. We will cease to dwell on the past. We will understand the true meaning of trust and love. No matter how much we have hurt our children, we will see that we can help them to heal. We will comprehend, and know how to apply, the curative powers of love, honesty, forgiveness, and faith. That feeling of isolation and inadequacy will disappear. We will lose our self-focus and learn to appreciate the needs and feelings of our children. Our whole approach to child raising will change. Fear of intimacy will leave us. We will solve problems we used to avoid. We will model respect and acceptance, and discover that our children will respond in kind. We will suddenly realize that we are doing for our families what we could never do for ourselves.

The possibility of leading your family to health and happiness may seem as daunting now as the possibility of a life without drugs seemed back then. Many parents once felt as overwhelmed as you may feel now. But they applied the principles of one-day-at-a-time parenting and were amazed at the results. I asked a group of parents how they have changed since recovery. Here are some of their responses:

"I've become more loving, more willing to accept that we have problems, and more confident they will be solved."

"I've become less selfish and less inclined to see the children as people to fulfill my needs. I try to listen and not direct their lives."

"I've learned to talk and discuss things from an admission of powerlessness, from the position of not being necessarily 'right.' I weigh, and watch the kids weigh, the pros and cons before a decision is reached. This has increased communication and brought us closer."

One mother of four offered this "promise" to recovering parents:

"You will learn to love, and you will find out that that's more important than being loved."

These parents spoke repeatedly of becoming more tolerant, patient, empathic, and accepting. Where they were once erratic, mean, and uncontrolled, they are now more consistent, loving, and responsible. Where they were once authoritarian and rejecting, they are now more open-minded and nurturing.

As parents apply the principles of recovery to family relationships, they witness consistently remarkable, and remarkably consistent, results: greater trust and cohesiveness, improved communication, clearer values, more effective problem solving, heightened sensitivity to the needs and feelings of others. How do these improvements in family dynamics affect the children of recovering parents?

"My kids trust me more. They talk about their problems."

"They're happier. They don't cower when I walk into the room. They invite their friends over."

"I've seen a lot of growth in their confidence and willingness to be affectionate."

"They're developing a lot of interests and intellectual curiosity. Maybe it's because they're free to put their energy into their own growth. I'd also like to think that my being there for them has encouraged them to take risks."

The most poignant and powerful testimony to the benefits of one-day-at-a-time parenting, however, comes from the children themselves. I asked kids of recovering parents for their thoughts on how their parents have changed since recovery. Here are some of their comments:

"My father's more calm."

"He treats me like his equal."

"He listens to what I have to say."

"He doesn't hit me anymore."

"He's gotten thinner."

"My father has changed a lot. He doesn't do stupid things and he doesn't stay out till 3:00 A.M. He does more things with the family."

"My mother has more energy and disciplines us more—in a good way, not like just yelling all the time. She doesn't sleep all the time like she used to."

"She treats us better than she used to."

"She talks to me."

What have these changes meant for their families?

"My parents don't fight the way they used to."

"I don't have to worry that my father is going to hurt us."

"I think we have a little more money even though it seems like we've been in debt forever."

I asked these same kids how *they* have changed as a result of their parents' recovery.

"I'm more relaxed since we get along better."

"I feel good about my mother."

"I don't hate my dad."

"I have become more aware of other people."

"I do better in school, talk a lot more, and every day I feel good about myself."

These healthy sentiments are supported by a growing body of research that suggests that recovery leads to positive changes in parenting methods and family functioning.

A study I recently conducted investigated differences in self-reported child-rearing practices and family functioning between alcoholic fathers and recovering alcoholic fathers. The study revealed statistically significant differences in family functioning ($p < .005$) between the two groups in all areas measured (e.g., family roles, values, communication, task accomplishment, and emotional involvement). Alcoholic fathers rated their family functioning in the "disturbed" range on seven out of the eight clinical scales; recovering fathers rated their families in the "normal" range on all eight clinical scales. This finding, well supported by other research, sends a message of hope to parents in recovery: You *can* become a better parent; your family *can* change and heal itself.

The study also found that alcoholic fathers were significantly more authoritarian in their child-rearing practices than were recovering fathers. Correlations showed this restrictive parenting style to be negatively associated with healthy family functioning. In other words, the more authoritarian a father reported his parenting style to be, the less healthy his family's functioning. A more nurturing parenting style was positively associated with healthy family functioning in such domains as emotional expression and involvement, values, discipline, decision making, and problem-solving styles.

Parents who live the principles of recovery at home practice a parenting style that is warm, accepting, and child centered. Such parents encourage their children—by attitude and deed—toward greater responsibility, trustworthiness, and empathy. They foster their children's autonomy and creativity. An abundance of research into the effects on children of child-rearing variations consistently shows that parents who practice one-day-at-a-time parenting methods are more likely than authoritarian or permissive parents to raise children who are friendly, cheerful, achieving, socially competent, and self-reliant.[2]

The alcoholics' ability to abstain from drinking affects the health of their family—at the same time that the health of their family affects their ability to abstain from drinking. Thus, family functioning and recovery from alcoholism appear to be intertwined in what can be patterns of either positive or negative reinforcement.[3]

This is an important point for parents in recovery. Sometimes we feel a conflict between our own recovery and the needs of our loved ones. There may be resentment from our spouse or children for all the time we spend at meetings or with program friends. Of course our own recovery must come first; we're no use to anyone if we can't stay clean and sober. However, recovering parents whose family remains mired in hurtful and ineffective patterns will have a harder time staying sober than recovering parents whose family joins them in working toward healthier attitudes and behaviors. This is common sense. Relapse feeds on tension, conflict, anger, and mistrust. Recovery feeds on serenity, problem solving, love, and support. Helping our family helps us. We put our own recovery first when we address the needs of others.

The promises offered in this chapter are real. You can become a better parent. You can bring trust, love, openness, and honesty into your family. No one's saying it will be easy. But you've already seen one miracle take place in your life.

Whether you credit yourself, your program, your friends, or your Higher Power for your recovery, these same forces are ready and able to create a new miracle for you as a parent. As you set off on this adventure, there are three words you should keep in mind: *Easy does it.*

3

Easy Does It

"I always assumed that as soon as I stopped drinking, my marriage would straighten out, my kids would look up to me, and we'd be one happy family again. What I found was a lot of resentment and mistrust. I had expected to be treated like a hero returning from the war, and instead I was treated like a deserter."

This recovering parent's experience is not unusual. If we are to succeed in rebuilding our families and restoring our relationships, we must take it one step at a time, one day at a time. *Easy does it.* This caution is particularly important for those in early recovery, whose eagerness to make up for lost time renders them especially vulnerable to unrealistic and self-defeating expectations. We must realize that our partner and children also need to recover, and that their pace and issues will be different from our own.

Your recovery as a parent is going to be threatened—and supported—by the same feelings and character traits that affect your personal recovery: resentment, shame, grandiosity, as well as humility, compassion, and love. There will be times when you will experience the glow of being clean, sober, and clearheaded; when you will feel understood and understanding, loved and loving; when you will know your family is on the mend.

And just as you begin to think: *Maybe this parenting bit isn't as hard as they say,* the ghost of past behaviors and emotions will return to rattle your relationships with fights, tears, and traumas.

You'll feel incompetent and depressed. It'll be enough to make you want to take a . . . a bath. *Easy does it.*

Your best defense against the ups and downs of family recovery is knowing what to expect. Here is a picture of some of the feelings and behaviors you and your family are likely to encounter.

Your family may experience a period of shared euphoria in the weeks or months immediately following your treatment or initial sobriety. Why? Because the dream has finally come true! You've stopped using. Now that you've quit, everything *has to be* all right. Your spouse or partner and children fall all over themselves to take care of you. Relief reigns as the daily horrors of active addiction are over. From now on it's going to be one happy family. Yea, right.

For underneath the pasted-on smiles and the grand expectations smolder the fears, hurts, and resentments that have built up over the years. Slowly, the belief that "everything will be all right once you quit" is proven wrong. Long-suppressed feelings rise to the surface. Family members have their own agendas and needs. Sharp words are exchanged. Sarcastic asides are made. And the fear of relapse has a chokehold on everybody's mind.

When you put on a new suit of sobriety and announce, "I'm ba-ack," you bring a stranger into the house. Your children don't know who or what to expect. They may tiptoe around in fear of "causing" a relapse. They may resent the time you spend at Twelve Step meetings. They may refuse to allow you into their lives.

Your spouse or partner, having assumed so much responsibility in your "absence," may be reluctant to relinquish it. He may be carrying years of bitterness and mistrust. He may resent the kids' forgiveness of you. In the eyes of the children, you were sick; but what was his excuse for being the disciplinarian, for being irritable, impatient, and preoccupied?

You may feel that your family doesn't applaud your courage loudly enough: *Don't they know what I'm going through? Don't they know that I'd do anything if only I could erase the past?* Apparently not. Their attitude is "It's about time," rather than "Hail to the

Chief." In fact, they are angry and resentful, which makes you angry and resentful.

Mixed in with your resentment is an increasing sense of responsibility for the suffering and anxiety your dependence has caused. You may try to pay off your guilt with lavish gifts and leniency. Or you may compensate for having abrogated your parenting role by becoming overly authoritarian. Such sudden turnabouts will be disorienting and distressing, not only to your children but also to your spouse or partner.

Now that addiction no longer rules the roost, your family's preexisting alliances and coping strategies are obsolete. As you struggle with new feelings, fantasies, and problems, unspoken questions will dominate your thoughts:

Will my family ever forgive me?
Can I earn back the respect, trust, and love of my children?
Will the guilt I feel ever go away?
How do I face my children's friends and teachers?
Will my spouse let me assume the responsibilities I neglected?

Your children will ask themselves:
Is Dad going to stay sober?
How come he's still grumpy and depressed?
Does he love me?
Will he remember the things I said and did?
Is he going to boss me around?
Will Mom and Dad still fight?
Is it safe to ask my friends over now?
Does he think it was all my fault?
What are we going to say to each other?

Your spouse or partner will wonder:
What if he relapses?
How is he going to treat the children?
How are the children going to react to him?
Is he going to undermine my relationship with the kids?

Are we going to have a social life now? A sex life?
Can I trust him with the finances?
Is he ever going to stop going to those meetings and start spending
some time at home?

What is it going to take for your family to address these daunting questions and issues? Trust, honesty, patience, open-mindedness, and healthy communication patterns. In other words, it's going to take everything most alcoholic families don't have. Family members have learned to avoid problems, to deny feelings, and to withdraw from one another and the world. They have adopted self- and other destructive roles in order to tend to their own and their family's survival.

You and your family have gone through a lifetime's worth of guilt, fear, and pain. While much of your misery is held in common, it has also affected each of you in different ways. You will best be able to help your children with their own healing if you recognize the profound sense of loss they are likely to feel now that you are in recovery.

Why should they feel a sense of loss? Because your recovery has thrown their world out of kilter. A family is a system, like a mobile: If one element moves, changes, or is put under stress, all elements move, change, or are put under stress. Your addiction defined your household environment. It shaped your family's rituals and routines. It provided each family member with a role and an identity, and, at times, an alibi. Your addiction became a handy scapegoat for *all* family problems, from financial difficulties to bad grades. And while your addiction may have contributed to or caused problems in these areas, it does not absolve other family members of their own responsibilities for creating and/or perpetuating them.

Loss, even of painful, hated burdens, requires a readjustment. Imagine a family that has oriented its life around caring for a parent who has been in a coma for years. Suddenly the parent recovers. Now people can get on with their lives. But what are those lives? For years they were defined by daily trips to the hospital, role contortions to take over the "missing" parent's responsibilities, coping strategies to deal with (or deny) emotional pain. With the horror of illness and uncertainty gone, a new uncertainty takes its place: *How will our family spend its time now? What will mealtimes, holidays, and vacations be like now? How will relationships change?*

Your recovery eliminates some of your family's most serious problems. But it also clears the way for new ones. Family members must now confront, individually and collectively, many of the issues and conflicts they have denied or ignored over the years. This is not to say that wreckage is all that you will find.

"My greatest fear," said one mother, "was that my children would hate me." Happily for this mother, they didn't. In fact, their reaction to her recovery was different than she'd expected: "They didn't care as much as I thought they would. They didn't react to the drama—the tragedy—of recovery as sympathetically as I'd imagined. I'm thankful now, but wasn't for ages."

Another recovering parent found this reaction from his two teenagers: "They were accepting and genuinely unsurprised by the twist of events. They were more sympathetic to my daily struggles than I would have thought, although they were somewhat too quick to agree with my newfound modesty—nodding their heads knowingly and vigorously when I took my own inventory out loud."

Many parents are amazed at the compassion and perceptivity with which their families respond to the changes wrought by recovery. Such parents speak of children who welcome them with affection and forgiveness, who are more resilient and less damaged than they had dared hope. Such stories are not offered to provide a false sense of hope or an excuse for neglecting to confront the hurt and dysfunction that have infected your family. Rather, they are meant to suggest that you are likely to find a range of reactions to your recovery. Some of your children may be less affected by your addiction than others. Some may be more forgiving and flexible. There will be times when your family will make strong, steady progress in its healing and other times when growth will slow, stop, or even seem to be going backward. *Easy does it.*

It's going to take a lot of time and effort for you and your family to adjust to a new way of life. You will need to learn to forgive, to negotiate, to provide growing room for one another, and to have fun. You will need to learn to express feelings and set limits.

The one-day-at-a-time parenting methods described in this book will help you to fill the void your recovery has created with trust, intimacy, and kind, honest communication. It's going to take time and work. But it will happen. Just remember: Home wasn't built in a day!

4

If You Want What We Have

Change is frightening. We don't want to let go of where we are—even if where we are makes us miserable—unless we can be sure we'll end up someplace better. Yet all change begins with willingness—to risk, to fail, to succeed. Trying to grow without it would be like expecting to get to the other side of a lake without shoving off from the dock.

The journey from willfulness to willingness has been critical to our own recovery—willingness to consider the existence of a power greater than ourselves; to examine our lives with rigorous honesty; to make amends; to ask for help. And we know that we are going to have to be willing to take risks and embrace change if our children and family relationships are to recover. Why, then, do we sit for weeks or months with willing intentions, without ever taking the first step toward putting them into practice?

It all comes down to the four-letter *f*-word: fear.

If you think about it, fear has probably been the greatest constant in our lives. If we grew up in an alcoholic family, we learned at an early age to be afraid. We were afraid of being rejected, beaten, or abused. We were afraid to trust and love, to get close to anyone, to bring friends to our house. We were so afraid of our powerful emotions that we learned to feel nothing.

Children are confronted daily with a parade of new and unknown sights, sounds, feelings, and experiences. These can be soothing, startling, delighting, disturbing. Imagine how an infant feels as she takes her first bath, her first taste of carrots, her first ride in a car. Imagine what the four-year-old feels on his first day of nursery school; the eight-year-old on his first night away from home; the fifteen-year-old on his first date. Out of these experiences, and the degree of love and support the child receives as he encounters them, develops the child's sense of himself and the world. Does he see the world as a place full of promise and challenge or danger and humiliation? Is it something he will conquer or be conquered by?

Not surprisingly, children who are highly creative and self-confident tend to be intrigued and excited by the unknown, rather than afraid of it. They want to dive in and figure things out. They are willing to take appropriate risks. They are *willing*. This doesn't mean that they are impervious to being hurt or disappointed. But they don't internalize failure as a sign of worthlessness.

Children who do not believe in their ability to meet new situations withdraw from the world. They assume defeat before they're at the starting gate (if they even step up to it in the first place); often they take refuge in alcohol and other drugs.

I remember a trip I took to Europe during college. I had just taken a train from Paris to Amsterdam to meet up with a friend from school, one of several with whom I had made the same arrangement: We would travel together until we couldn't stand each other anymore. I met my friend outside the train station, and we headed to our hotel. Ah, Holland—land of flowers, canals, and cafes—I took a deep breath and inhaled the wonderful smells of the city: fresh-baked pastries, marijuana, hashish.

I had been looking forward to trying *rijsttafel,* the Indonesian banquet famous in Amsterdam (and presumably in Indonesia as well), which consists of rice served with tasting-sized portions of dozens of delicacies. Smorgasbords appealed to my personality; you could have everything. We walked up and down the colorful streets while engaging in my second favorite activity in the world: deciding where to eat dinner. Each restaurant tried to outdo the next as it boasted of the number of dishes included in its feast. At this point in my life, the notion that *less is more* had not yet become an operative construct; so, with *more is more* as my guide, I set my saliva on a lovely-looking restaurant that advertised a Glutton Special of 428 different dishes and thirty gallons of rice for a negligible number of guilders. I noted that the *rijsttafel* banquets were only served to two or more people. No problem. I was certain my friend would want to indulge as well.

"Do you want to go in here?" I asked.

"Sure," he replied.

"I can't wait to try this *rijsttafel* thing."

"But it's only for two people."

"So?" I said, as a shadow of doom crept across my culinary consciousness.

"So," he said, "I don't want it."

Well, you could have knocked me over with a tulip. The shock of it all—that someone else wasn't seeing the world through my eyes, that all taste buds didn't work according to the standards set by mine.

"How can you not want it?" I asked with my usual tolerance.

"I just don't," he said.

"But why not?" I pressed. He could have said almost anything— "I tried it once and I hated it"; "I'm not hungry"; "I've been dying for a steak all day"—and I would have (grudgingly) accepted it.

But the reason he gave for not wanting to try the *rijsttafel* was this: "Because I might not like it."

Because I might not like it. How sad, I thought. *If he won't try a few bites of food because he might not like it, how does he deal with higher-risk situations?* Our respective willingnesses to try new things led, not surprisingly, to a travel divorce a few days later on the grounds of digestive incompatibility. (Can you believe he wanted to eat three full meals a day?) I continued to keep in touch with this friend over the years. I saw again and again the extent to which fear controlled his choices and limited his life (not that I was taking his inventory or anything). Eventually, my friend found his way to a Twelve Step program (although it was not, I might add, one for eating disorders, which is what I certainly would have advised after our experience in Amsterdam).

This fear that we "might not like it" keeps us from moving and growing. How many times have we looked over the menu in a restaurant (if you will excuse my continuing preoccupation with food) and asked ourselves: *Do I try something new or stick with what I like?* For alcoholics, however, the question is just as likely to be: *Do I try something new or stick with what I* don't *like?*

Recovery is like walking up a down escalator. If we stand still, we go backward. Going forward means being willing to confront our fears, to accept them, and to act in spite of them.

And what are some of these fears? I have asked this question of many recovering parents, often getting similar answers:

"I was afraid of having to look at the destruction my addiction had caused."

"My biggest fear was that my kids wouldn't love me and that I'd be a terrible failure as a parent."

"My biggest fear," said a mother of two, "was that I wouldn't like my children. I know that sounds like an awful thing to say, but because I had always seen their needs as interfering with my drinking and my conscience, I had it in my head that they were the problem."

"I was terrified that I would say or do the wrong thing and all the progress we had made as a family would be destroyed."

"I was afraid of getting close to my kids. One, because I didn't know how, and two, because I figured they wouldn't respect me if they knew what I was really like."

One parent volunteered this fear: "I was most afraid of having a relapse. I was sure that if it happened, my kids would never trust me again. It would be a betrayal we wouldn't be able to survive. I think it was that fear that kept me sober."

This parent's comment raises an important point: *Fear is not necessarily bad.* Fear, like pain, is a warning light nature places on the dashboard of our awareness. It tells us to take action or to not take action. It keeps us from hurting ourselves or others. The fear of hurting our children can help us to be more responsible and empathic. The goal of recovery is not to rid our lives of fear, but rather, to learn to handle fear—to know it and name it—so that it doesn't paralyze us.

If we are willing to change our attitudes and behaviors, the parenting methods discussed throughout this book will eliminate many of the fears we feel as parents. We will know how to handle situations that used to baffle us. Instead of fearing conflict, we will deal with it. Instead of fearing guilt, we will let go of it. Instead of fearing rejection, we will keep coming back. Instead of fearing intimacy, we will learn how to communicate.

Most fears are of our own making—and therefore can be unmade. They are the result of projection, mistrust, grandiosity. By sharing our fears with others, we will see that we are not the only parents who feel hurt, confused, unworthy, unloving, unlovable. And we will see that the key to overcoming the fears that stand in the way of good parenting is willingness.

A Parent's Declaration of Willingness

- I am willing to acknowledge my worth as a parent and individual.
- I am willing to believe that I have a priceless gift to give to my child.
- I am willing to love my child unconditionally.
- I am willing to accept my child as a unique individual with the right to her own thoughts, feelings, interests, and dreams.
- I am willing to let go of my need to control.
- I am willing to turn my worries over to a Higher Power.
- I am willing to listen as well as talk.

- I am willing to express my own feelings.
- I am willing to be flexible and to risk change.
- I am willing to take a searching and fearless inventory of my parenting attitudes and methods.
- I am willing to look for ways in which my character defects affect my parenting.
- I am willing to ask for help.

Part Two

To Practice These Principles

5

One Day at a Time
Giving Our Children the Gift of Today

. . . Our lives had become unmanageable.

That feeling of powerlessness stays imprinted in our memories forever. It is good that it does so. It helps to keep us straight and sober.

We were out of control when we were using. We raged against the world—licking our wounds, counting our grievances. Our salvation always lay in the future: *Once we have more money . . . ; Once we fall in love . . . ; Once we move to the country . . . ; Once people stop bugging us . . .* everything would be all right.

By living in the past and the future, we created a void in the present. We learned in recovery how to fill that void: by living in today.

We take things one day at a time now. One moment at a time. The future is something we protect rather than something we project. The past enlightens rather than entraps us. We may, however, still use the past as a weapon against our kids. We remind them of their mistakes; we stick shaming labels on them that can last a lifetime; we become so focused on what they used to be like that we fail to recognize what they are like now:

"How could you have been so stupid?"

"Last year I let you go and look what happened."

"I'll remember this the next time you want something."

Not only do we hold the past over our kids' heads, but we use it to predict their future. We worry and build expectations and then orient the lives of our children around these fears and goals—around *our* fears and goals.

"If you don't buckle down, you're never going to amount to anything."

"How do you expect to make any friends if you spend all your time on the computer?"

What does it mean to take things one day at a time with our kids?

Said one parent: "I don't try to cover my child's entire academic career every time I'm asked for help with homework. I just answer the question—and smile."

Said another: "I try not to push my kids to pursue future goals as the only worthwhile thing. I try to make 'now' good for us all, even in times of conflict."

Many parents speak of another type of reward that comes from staying in the moment. One mother said it well: "I've gotten to know my children so much better. This is because I'm much more interested in what they're doing and feeling now than in what they're going to do or feel a week, a year, or five years from now. It's amazing how much less there is to nag and worry about when I replace my fears with a little faith."

When we look out for our children's present, we *are* looking out for their future. It is the quality of today—the quality of our home environment, relationships, and parenting that determines how our children feel about themselves, about others, and about their ability to meet what life brings their way. Of course, we need to plan and prepare: to see that our children are vaccinated as infants, to save for their education, to provide opportunities for their growth. But the most important foundation for the future is built moment by moment. Every day presents a new occasion for us to model integrity, to deal positively with stress and conflict, to support friends and family, to help our children develop confidence and self-esteem.

Staying in the day isn't easy. One recovering parent recalled with humor an example from his past: "Before my kids even went to school I worried about what kind of students they'd be. When they were in first grade, I worried about who their second grade teacher would be. When they were in junior high, I worried about their SAT scores. When they were in high school, I worried about whether they'd get into a good college. Finally, my oldest son goes off to an Ivy League college. My worries are over. So what does he do? He drops out after a year. So much for *my* plans."

This father was bemused that, in all the time he spent laying out his son's life, he neglected one little thing: what his son wanted, who his son was. "All those years of worry, what a waste. I bet if you did a study of everything parents worry about and everything that actually happens to their kids, the things parents worry about are rarely the things that end up happening."

Teaching our children to live one day at a time is one of the greatest gifts we can offer them. For our children, like us, begin to hurt when they leave the present. It is when they labor under an unresolved burden from the past that they feel resentful, guilty, or ashamed. It is when they worry and despair about the future that they feel depressed, frightened, or unmotivated.

Teaching our children to take life one day at a time means teaching them to be patient and accepting, to have faith and perspective. It means encouraging them to take good care of themselves, to seek progress rather than perfection, to break great dreams—and mundane obligations—into manageable steps. Children who live one day at a time learn from their errors rather than flee from them. They create goals for themselves rather than obstacles.

This approach to life is a tall order for anyone. We have seen in our own lives what a delicate balance it is to learn from the past, plan for the future, and live in the present. But we have found that this is how we grow, find serenity, and take care of ourselves and others.

How do we teach our children to live one day at a time? Implicitly, by setting an example with our own lives and explicitly, by encouraging certain behaviors and attitudes. We will see how to do this over the course of this book.

We can bring to each moment with our children the quality of interaction and emotion that best prepares them for the future if we practice the following one-day-at-a-time parenting principles:

Today I will love my child without condition. I will recognize that the best way to help my child grow and change is to love him as he is. I will remember that my job as a parent is to find my child's strengths, not his weaknesses.

Today I will accept myself. I will forgive myself for mistakes I have made as a parent. I will recognize the priceless gift of love that only I can give to my child.

Today I will accept the circumstances of my family. I will understand that there is a reason for any pain or conflict we may experience. I will believe that its purpose is not to defeat our family but to help us become stronger and more loving.

Today I will choose how to react. I will not be a puppet on my child's strings. I will recognize anger, resentment, worry, or hurt as something of my own making.

Today I will not regret the past. If I look back, it will be to learn from my errors in order that I may act with greater understanding.

Today I will not worry about the future. I will not project the rest of my child's life onto the events of today. I will not torment myself over things I cannot control. I will take action where appropriate. All else I will put in the hands of my Higher Power.

Today I will live in the present. While I will make amends for the past and plan for the future, I will embrace the day as if it might be my last. I will cherish this opportunity to be with and learn from my family.

Today I will be responsible. I will honor my commitments and keep my promises. I will do everything possible to see that my child's physical, practical, emotional, and spiritual needs are met.

Today I will deal with conflict. I will recognize that conflict is natural and healthy. I will not try to win arguments. I will try to solve problems.

Today I will be honest with myself and my family. I will take responsibility for accepting and dealing with my emotions. I will communicate my feelings and needs to my family, and encourage them to do the same.

Today I will not try to control my child's life. I will not presume to direct my child's interests, feelings, and relationships. I will provide my child with the love, values, and limits he needs to feel secure and to fulfill his destiny as a unique human being.

Today I will ask for help. If I am in any way harming or abusing my child, I will ask others to help me and to help my child. I will recognize this as a moral imperative.

Today I will be grateful. I will reflect upon the wondrous miracle of my child. I will count my blessings.

Today I will model the kindness, understanding, and respect I would like to receive from my children. I will remember that what I do has far greater impact on my child than what I say.

Today I will maintain my serenity. I will be calm in the face of family chaos, optimistic in the face of family conflict.

Today I will consider my child my equal. I will respect my child's unique identity and her worth as a person. I will grant her the right to mature at her own pace and in her own way. I will not try to own or manipulate her. I will recognize that age and experience mean nothing in the eyes of my Higher Power.

Today I will not try to solve all my child's problems. I will offer love, support, and counsel. But I will not deprive my child of the opportunity to make her own decisions and solve her own problems. I will give my child the gift of my faith in her abilities.

Today I will learn something from my child. I will recognize that my child is my greatest teacher. If I listen carefully, she will tell me what I need to know.

6

And When We Were Wrong
Making Amends to Our Children

The fifteen-year-old son of a practicing alcoholic was telling me about a recent exchange he had had with his father. The boy paced the room, chasing his anger.

"How can I be so dumb?" he said, shaking his head. "Every time, I swear I'll never do it again. I'll never tell him another thing as long as I live. But then he puts on his Mr. Calm and Reasonable act like he really cares what I think, and my mother puts on this fake sweet voice—like the two of them actually agree on something, which would be a real laugh—and they say: 'How can we help if we don't know what's bothering you?' So I begin to think, *Well, maybe they do care, like maybe it'll be different this time.* So I tell them what's bothering me and—it's like someone tells you to hold out your hand so they can shake it and when you do—ZAP—they cut it off."

"Tell me what happened," I said.

The boy sat down and sighed. "A few nights ago I was at hockey practice and it was my dad's turn to pick me and my friends up. So it's ten o'clock and he doesn't show, and we wait and wait and everyone's pissed at me and finally my mom picks us up like an hour late. So the next day the Great Hungover One comes down to breakfast and I say, 'How come you didn't pick us up last night?' and he gives me this dirty look.

"Every little thing I do, he's always on my case, but when he screws up it's as if it never happened. And my mother goes right along with it. So over the next few days I kind of gave them the silent treatment, which is why they wanted to know what was bothering me. So like a stupid idiot I took the bait."

"What did you say?"

"I said to my father, 'How come, whenever I do something wrong, you make such a big deal about it, but in all the years I've known you, you've never once admitted making a mistake?'

"So my father's chin gets all twitchy, and he says real slowly through his teeth: 'That's because I haven't made any!'"

Although this incident represented just the tip of the iceberg in terms of the family's problems, the boy's anger and frustration were easy to understand.

Fathers as a species can't admit that they are wrong and ask for forgiveness any more than they can admit that they are lost and ask for directions. And *addicted* fathers—and mothers—are even less likely to acknowledge their errors. This is due, in part, to our basic stance of denial toward our addiction and its consequences. To admit even one wrongdoing is to open the door to a thousand. So it's easier to keep the focus on others' mistakes and, when bludgeoned by reality into an inescapable admission of guilt, to offer an insincere apology while whispering to ourselves that it's really everyone else's fault.

We have seen how this avoidance of responsibility harmed us when we were using. In recovery, we learn that making amends is one of the most spiritually cleansing acts we can undertake. When we scour the past in search of people we have harmed, we are forced to review and renew our relationships. Nowhere is this more vital than with our children. The recovery of family trust and communication depends on it.

As parents in recovery, we may balk at making amends to our children. We do this for the usual reasons—shame, self-justification, fear of rejection—but also for reasons specific to the parent-child relationship.

"What I did to my child when I was drinking," said one recovering mother, "was so unacceptable, I can't bear to bring it up. I don't want to put my child through it again." Our children's youth and innocence, plus the irretrievability of lost years, make these wrongs committed against them especially painful to confront. One can understand why this mother didn't want to "put her child through it again." But perhaps what she really felt was: I *don't want to have to go through it again.*

When we were using, our addiction was "the elephant in the middle of the room" that nobody talked about. If, in recovery, we refuse to admit and redress our wrongs, we are turning the *consequences* of our addiction into another "invisible elephant" messing up the family room. If our children were able to survive our sarcasm or slaps, they will be able to survive our amends. Making amends to children does not plunge them into the mire of the past. Rather, it pulls them out of it. When the past is brought out into the open, children can begin to feel: *I* wasn't *crazy; it* wasn't *my fault; my mom* shouldn't *have hit me.* Making amends allows our children to forgive us—a critical step in their healing and ours.

Some parents may be reluctant to admit their wrongs due to pride or the belief that such admissions undermine authority. Nothing could be further from the truth. We undermine our authority when we present ourselves as infallible. This is because what we're really showing our kids is not perfection but hypocrisy and false pride. The fifteen-year-old boy whose father denied ever making a mistake knows that his father makes mistakes all the time (and that *he* knows it). Thus, the statement, in its dishonesty and absurdity, demeans the father even further in his son's eyes. When we present ourselves as human—mistakes and all—our kids are going to trust and respect us more. They will be more likely to confide in us and to admit their own mistakes. Whether we laugh or cry at our errors, as long as we admit them, we provide our children with a wonderful model for honesty, humility, and growth.

Making Amends to Children

The process of making amends to children begins by conducting a "searching and fearless moral inventory of ourselves."[4] We can do this by examining our past behaviors and attitudes in terms of several broad categories.

Making Amends for Character Defects That Harmed Our Children

If we were to outline our wrongdoings, character defects would provide the headings. Some of these character defects assaulted our kids with tidal force: the anger that unleashed a storm of abuse or the perfectionism that pelted stinging and incessant criticism. Other defects, such as dishonesty, selfishness, or irritability, harmed them more slowly, less spectacularly, like the steady drip of water that, over time, wears away even the hardest surface. Bit by bit these defects eroded our children's trust, self-esteem, and happiness.

"I had a hard time figuring out how to make amends to my child," said a recovering mother. "It wasn't as though I could put my finger on a few terrible things I had done and make up for them. It wasn't what I had done, but how I had been, *who* I had been. My character defects had harmed my child. So I made a list of them. And then for each one, I wrote down its opposite. So when I wrote *critical,* I matched it with *accepting.* And *irritable* became *good-natured.* I used the positive side of my list as a blueprint for making amends."

This mother also made an explicit apology to her children. "I wanted them to know that I was sorry that I hadn't been the type of mother I wanted to be. It was important that I not just sweep it under the rug. I also didn't want them to think it was their fault."

Children of addicted parents often think that it *is* their fault, that *they* must be bad or unlikable, because why else would their parents yell at them, hit them, or ignore them? An explicit apology helps to free kids from this type of guilt. Without the apology, a child might assume that "Mom's nicer because I'm not as bad as I used to be." The child needs a context in which to understand changes in his parent's way of relating to him. The apology creates this context and marks the starting point for healing.

Keep in mind that amends must reflect your child's current age and circumstances. You cannot turn the clock back to make up for lost years. One recovering father spoke about this painful truth: "I drank away my son's childhood. I didn't come into the program until he was sixteen. I missed it all—his first tooth, his first day of school, his first bike, his first date. As soon as I had some sobriety under my belt, I wanted more than anything to be a real father to my kid. I had this image we'd play catch and go camping and roughhouse on the floor and I'd talk to him about girls and life and take him to basketball games. I've had a real hard time dealing with the fact that a lot of those things aren't going to happen, that my kid's grown beyond them. He's got other interests; he's found other adults to rely on."

This, of course, is one of the great tragedies of addiction for both parents and children. Lost years are lost. This father dealt with his pain and grief, and eventually accepted the reality of his (and his son's) loss. Now he is building a relationship with his son, whom he recognizes not as a surrogate seven-year-old but as a mature sixteen-year-old. And he does so with the knowledge that there won't be any more lost years if he stays away from that first drink.

Making Amends for Patterns of Behavior That Harmed Our Children

Another way of identifying wrongs we committed against our children is to look for behavior patterns such as breaking promises, forgetting commitments, being perpetually late. Perhaps we gave our kids daily lectures on their faults. We may have cast them into inappropriate roles, which resulted in their assuming responsibilities that should have been ours (cooking, cleaning, closing the house up at night) or that shouldn't have been—period (lying on our behalf, putting us to bed, protecting siblings from abuse).

A mother who'd been in a Twelve Step program for a year described the role reversal and resultant behavior patterns that took place in her family. "During the last three years of my addiction, things got so bad that I could barely drag myself out of the house to work. God only knows how I managed that. From the time she was ten, my daughter got her brothers up in the morning, fixed their breakfast, made their lunches, took them shopping, and helped with their homework. Because I'm a single parent, you'd expect the oldest child to have more responsibilities than in a two-parent family. But this went way beyond that. Even when I was acting as the mommy, it was usually at my daughter's instigation.

"Several months into recovery, I vowed to myself that I was going to give my daughter her childhood back—what was left of it. This was the first amend I needed to make. What I wasn't prepared for was how much she resisted the change."

This mother's experience is not unusual. Children get cast into roles by their parents' addiction. These roles, even if they are burdensome or inappropriate, become part of the child's identity and security. In this case, the daughter's assumption of parental responsibilities was a way of coping with, and escaping from, the family's problems. It maintained her sense of self-respect, the bonds of affection with her brothers, and, possibly, the hope that Mom would get better if she didn't have so much to do. The daughter had become the family "hero." She knew how to be a great mother. But she didn't know how to be a child. No wonder she resisted giving up her role. From her point of view, it was a slap in the face: Mom gets her act together, comes home, and says, "I'll take over now. Thanks for covering. You go run along and play."

The purpose of making amends is to undo errors, repair damage, and make ourselves and those we have wronged feel better. Fortunately, this mother was able to keep this recognition paramount. With the help of her sponsor, she was able to understand her daughter's perspective and to incorporate it into the solution.

"I realized how much I owed my daughter for keeping our family together and functioning. I told her how much her helpfulness and responsibility had meant to me and her brothers. But I also told her that I was sorry she had had to take on the role of a parent when she was still a child and that I wanted her to be able to goof off and spend time with her friends without feeling guilty. Isn't that a switch!" laughed the mother. "I was probably the only parent on the planet telling my child to be *less* responsible.

"My daughter protested that she liked helping. We ended up making lists of all the things she did for me, for her brothers, and for herself. You can guess which list was shortest. I encouraged her to keep doing the things that were an 'older sister' part of her relationship with her brothers, like helping them with their homework. For other things I insisted on paying her, so that at least she would understand that I felt they were extra and not part of her normal chores. Maybe this sounds like a cumbersome approach, but it was the only way I could think of to make an amend without hurting her even more."

This approach doesn't sound cumbersome at all. It sounds wise, loving, and practical. Out of a broad wrongdoing—inappropriately thrusting an adult role upon a child—came a concrete amend that could be discussed and modified. As this mother recognized, making amends should never be a process of bending a child's will into a shape it doesn't want to go. The amend should be made to fit the child, not the other way around.

Making Amends for Unique Events That Harmed Our Children

When we take our moral inventory, we usually come up with a list of specific incidents for which we need to make amends. For example:

"I showed up drunk at my child's school open house."

"I threw my kid's Walkman out the window and broke it."

"I said terrible, hateful things to my son when he told me he was gay."

"I walked naked into my daughter's room when her friends were there. I thought it was the bathroom."

Some parents find these amends "easier" to make in that they stem from discrete events. The mother who came drunk to the open house apologized to her daughter and attended every school play, conference, and PTA meeting the next year squeaky clean and sober. The father who broke the Walkman apologized to his son and, as interest for the nine months in which the boy had been deprived of its use, not only replaced the unit but bought a pair of miniature speakers to go along with it. The father who excoriated his son for being gay couldn't erase the hurt he had caused. But he apologized, sought to learn about and understand homosexuality, became active in organizations for parents of gay children, and was ultimately able to love and accept his child.

Some wrongs are more difficult to redress. For example, what could the father who stumbled naked into his teenage daughter's room do to remove the stain he had cast upon her pride? In an attempt to make an amend for the incident, he offered to apologize directly to the girl's friends. His daughter cringed at the idea, saying that that would embarrass her even more. The father respected her wishes. The only way he could make amends for the incident was to acknowledge his regret and vow that he would never humiliate her like that again.

A recovering mother touched on an important point when she talked about amends she had made to her son. "I had prepared a little cue card so I wouldn't forget any of the things I wanted to say. I went through the list, apologizing and explaining and telling him how I wanted to make up for as many of them as possible. When I finished, there was this long silence, and then he said, 'Is that all?'

"'What do you mean?' I asked.

"'I mean, what about when you—?' And he went on to list about twenty other things I had done that I had no recollection of."

This mother's experience is particularly relevant to alcoholic parents who may have committed wrongs against their children during a blackout or at times when they were too inebriated to recall clearly what happened. This possibility can be addressed by asking your child if there are *other* incidents he would like to talk about, *other* things you did that hurt or angered him. It is important that you not place on your child the responsibility for seeking out your wrongs. You're not asking: "Is there anything you think I owe you an apology for?" Rather, you're saying: "If there are *other* things I did when I was drinking that upset you, I'd really appreciate the chance to talk about them and try to make up for them."

Invite your child to recall any events or interactions that she feels were hurtful or unfair. When you do so, remember that the customer—er, the child—is always right. You are the person making amends—not she. As incidents come out of the past, you may be tempted to argue or find fault with your child; to try to justify your behavior; to say, "Yes, but—" or "Wait a minute, you shouldn't have—."

Well, don't. Amends have nothing to do with whether your child was at fault. Amends address your side of the equation. And if your child was sullen, cruel, or selfish, perhaps some of the responsibility for that behavior rests with you.

Making Amends for Behavior That Indirectly Harmed Our Children

Many of our actions when using harmed our children even though these actions were not committed directly against them. For example, our gambling increased our children's feelings of insecurity. Our inability to keep a job meant we kept uprooting our kids from city to city. Losing our driver's license meant that our children had to curtail their extracurricular activities and social lives.

A fourteen-year-old boy shared a memory of an event that falls into this category of wrongdoing. "One night my dad was drunk and he beat my mom and gave her a black eye. So I hit him with a frying pan."

When I later asked this boy what one thing upset him most about his father's drinking, he said, "The time I hit him with a frying pan." Thus, the father's abuse, though not directed at his son, drew the boy into an emotionally painful situation that caused long-lasting guilt.

These types of events are ripe for the making of amends. This boy recounted his father's: "He apologized for hitting my mom. He said, 'I know I hurt you when I hurt your mother and I'm very sorry for it.' He hasn't hit her since he stopped drinking. He also said that I was right to protect my mom."

Making Amends for Physical, Sexual, or Emotional Abuse That Harmed Our Children

Physical, sexual, and/or emotional abuse of children is significantly more likely to occur in families with substance-abusing parents than in those without them. Thus, it would not be surprising if your inventory uncovered such incidents. Although in some circumstances adequate amends can be made, in many other cases, years of abuse cannot be undone with an apology or the passing of subsequent abuse-free years.

The potential for lifelong damage from the physical, emotional, or sexual abuse of children is such that I would urge parents who have committed these wrongs to seek outside help—for their children and for themselves. The child must have a safe environment in which to experience and talk about her feelings. It is unlikely that the perpetrator of the abuse can provide such an environment. Facilitate your child's access to professional counseling and/or support groups—her needs and rights come before your own. Keep in mind that there are laws and regulations governing the reporting of child abuse. School personnel, for example, are required to report cases of suspected or actual child abuse to authorities. As you and your family deal with these painful issues, you may wish to consult with an attorney to understand the ramifications of your past actions and current options.

Encouraging Children to Make Amends

Children, too, need to learn how to make amends. Doing so allows them to take responsibility for their actions and to expiate the guilt and regret they often feel as a result of their misdeeds.

The first amend most young children learn to make is a verbal apology. They discover that saying "I'm sorry" is a sure way to get out of trouble, avoid punishment, and put a smile back on Mommy's face. The challenge for parents is to help their children understand the meaning and purpose behind the words, so that saying "I'm sorry" becomes an expression of genuine regret rather than a reflexive shield against anger. Older children, for example, often say, "*I said* I'm sorry," conveying their expectation that that's all they need to do to set things right.

There are a number of things you can do to help your child understand that an apology is more than just words.

Identify the Offending Behavior

The apology of a very young child may simply be a learned behavior. She mouths the words because she knows it pleases her parents. When your child says "I'm sorry," ask her to describe the behavior for which she is apologizing. If your child says, "For taking the cookie," you can add: "Yes, taking your sister's cookie upset her and made her cry."

If your child draws a blank, verbalize the behavior yourself: "That's right. You said you're sorry because you pushed your friend and he hurt his knee. Now he knows that you feel bad that you hurt him."

Identifying the focus of the apology helps your child to make the link between the offending action and the damage or hurt it caused.

Build Empathy, not Shame

Let's say your child grabs a jar of paint out of his playmate's hand. The paint spills all over the friend's painting and the little boy begins to cry.

"Look what you've done!" you yell at your child. "You've ruined his painting. You apologize this minute."

This response fills your child with shame. He learns that he is a "bad boy." His apology is motivated by fear of punishment and a desire to appease you, rather than by a desire to help his friend get over his hurt.

A better response would be to focus on the action itself and its consequences:

"Jimmy is crying because you spilled paint on his painting. He spent a lot of time making it. I know you didn't mean to do it, but it still hurt Jimmy. I want you to tell Jimmy you're sorry so he knows you feel bad that his painting is ruined."

This approach helps your child to understand how his actions affect others. You can also help your child to develop empathy by recalling similar situations in which he was upset: "Do you remember how you felt when Mark broke your truck? I bet Jimmy feels like that now."

Help Your Child to Right the Wrong

As children mature, they need to learn that saying "I'm sorry" is often not enough. They need to assume responsibility for the consequences of their actions, to fix what they broke, to heal the hurt they caused. When the damage is physical, the amend is usually obvious: A child who writes on walls can help to wipe them off; a child who carelessly breaks a toy can contribute to the cost of a new one. Emotional damage is harder to redress. Ask your child for her ideas on ways to mend hurt feelings. A child who says nasty things to a friend could write her a letter. A child who teases a younger sibling could play a game with her.

Appropriate amends are not always clear. Human interactions are messy. Don't worry if the connection between offense and expiation isn't exact. The important thing is to give your child a chance to assume responsibility and heal hurt feelings.

Empathy and responsibility are cornerstones of moral behavior. In the next chapter the making of amends is presented as the basis for an entire system of discipline. We'll discuss why punishment has no place in one-day-at-a-time parenting and why children who admit their errors and take responsibility for the consequences of their actions learn self-control and good judgment.

7

Stop Playing God
Letting Our Children Assume
Responsibility for Their Lives

A friend of mine is fond of saying: "There are three types of people: (1) Those who believe in God; (2) Those who do not; and (3) Those who believe they *are* God." Most addicts probably belong to the third category. Especially where their kids are concerned.

When we were using, we tried to control everyone and everything around us. The world, however, had plans of its own and, to our great indignation, carried on without our divine intervention. Fortunately, there was one place where we could play God with somewhat better results: home sweet home. In this kingdom we were still boss. Listen to "God" speak:

"Because I'm your father and I said so!"

"You'll do as you're told!"

"I don't owe you an explanation."

"As long as you're living under my roof, you'll follow my rules!"

We used every trick in the book to get things our way: fear, guilt, love, withdrawal of love. The more out of control we got, the more we tried to control others. If only people did what we wanted, our troubles would disappear. Of course it never worked that way. Our attempts to impose order on the external world couldn't compensate for the internal chaos we felt.

In recovery, we learn that our need to control grows out of insecurity and fear. We learn that the belief that we can control people and things is irrational and self-destructive. We discover that our real power lies in recognizing our powerlessness. This frees us to work on ourselves and to let others work on themselves. If we don't have to control everyone else, we don't have to feel responsible for them either. What a relief!

So, we stop playing God. We let the weather carry on without our interference; we let relatives indulge their eccentricities without our judgments; we let colleagues go about their jobs without our instruction. But we find it awfully hard to stop playing God at home.

A parent's job is not to control his child. It is to care for his child. To nurture, nourish, protect, support, encourage, respect, and love his child. To those of you whose parental reflexes are twitching with objections—"But children have to have limits" and "What about rules?" and "How do children learn without being corrected?"—I'm getting to all that.

But before I do, I want to undermine one of the most fundamental beliefs of parenting: that the parent role in and of itself entitles the bearer to obedience. This belief, buried deep in the collective parental unconscious, is hogwash. Worse than that, it is dangerous—when it causes other adults to turn their back on an abusive situation lest they interfere with a parent's "right" to discipline his child, or when children themselves internalize the message that they are "bad" and must bear their parents' punishments without challenge.

Anyone can become a parent. All you have to do is—well, you've probably figured it out by now. Having a child can be an act of negligence, selfishness, treachery, or desperation. Once the child is born, parents can be cruel and abusive; they can fail to provide for their child's needs; they can, whether through ignorance or willfulness, subject their child to physical and emotional distress. So please, let's get rid of this idea that parents, simply because they are parents, automatically merit a child's respect and obedience.

Respect must be earned. When respect is demanded, it is not respect the child feels, but fear. Genuine respect grows out of admiration for the way a person behaves, thinks, and treats people; the principles she values; the judgment she shows. It is possible to love somebody without respecting her and to respect somebody without loving her.

Can we really say that we *deserved* our children's respect when we were using? When we were abrogating responsibilities, hurting feelings, and breaking promises? Hardly. We lost our children's respect. Now we must *earn* it back. And we will, now that our behavior and values are respectable.

The first step in earning back our children's respect is to reach deep inside ourselves and wrench out our old ideas about discipline. We need to abandon our concept of parent-child relationships as being grounded in the parent's supremacy and the child's subserviency. Once we get rid of these destructive concepts, we can begin to base our parental "authority" on mutual acceptance and respect. In recovery we discover that we become powerful when we admit our powerlessness. This paradox operates in the realm of parenting as well: The less we try to control our children, the more influential we will be. One way of understanding this paradox is by examining the relationship between a sponsor and his sponsee.

Be Your Child's Sponsor

Few people have exerted greater positive influence on our lives than our sponsors. Many of us owe our sobriety, our serenity, and our reentry into society to them. In fact, it is hard to imagine a greater bond of love and respect than that which unites a recovering addict to his sponsor. Did we come to feel this way because our sponsors demanded our respect and obedience? Because they told us what to feel, who to be, and how to behave? No. It was because they *didn't* do any of these things.

Then what did they do?

They accepted us unconditionally. They cared for us when we weren't able to care for ourselves. They modeled responsible behavior and decision making. They let us experience the consequences of our actions, even when they saw us heading in wrong directions. They gave us encouragement and support. They made us feel that they'd been where we were now, that they understood our fears and doubts. They pointed us toward our own resources. They listened. And they loved us, faults and all.

And what happened? Did we abuse their trust and confidence? No, we lived up to it. Did we become spoiled and selfish? No, we became more productive and responsible. Did we become lazy and unmotivated? No, we developed perseverance. We set goals. We learned tolerance and gratitude. We became fuller, healthier human beings.

We were children in recovery. And while our sponsors had more experience than we did, they never made us feel the lesser because of it. They modeled a life whose values and substance we admired. They helped us to see options, consider alternatives, and clarify feelings. They encouraged emotional honesty and straightforward communication. They were never selfish but they set limits—sensible limits, based not on equations of power and dominance, but on common sense, courtesy, and practicality. Isn't a good sponsor like a good parent? Isn't the type of growth our sponsors motivated in us the type of growth we wish to motivate in our children?

Our sponsors did not try to control us. They did not demand our obedience. In fact, if they had "parented" us with a fusillade of rules, we would never have learned to stand on our own two feet. This is because of one of the great paradoxes of parenting: *Fewer rules make for better behavior.* Since this idea flies in the face of everything we are taught about raising children, let's look at it more closely.

Fewer Rules Make for Better Behavior

On my first day as a school headmaster, one of the students approached me before school and handed me several sheets of paper. "These are the rules," he said rather glumly.

"Rules?"

"Yeah, rules. You know, don't pick your nose in class, no eating with your mouth full, that sort of thing."

I thanked the budding comedian and took the list to my office to examine. There were about fifty items of the no-food-in-the-common-room, no-bouncing-balls-in-the-hallway variety. I was surprised by the existence of such a list, since the school, a "free school," had been founded as an alternative to traditional schools with their endless rules and regimentation. This school was supposed to be democratic and student centered. Discipline was to be achieved through each student's self-control, understanding of community values, and respect for the rights of others. If I knew one thing about creating this type of warm, supportive, intellectually stimulating environment, it was that you *didn't* go about it with a three-page list of rules. I was determined to bring the issue up at an all-school meeting to see whether we couldn't arrive at some basis other than a list of rules for setting and maintaining standards of behavior.

I entered the common room and found the various components of the student body sprawled on rugs, slumped in chairs, and perched on bookshelves. "Do you know what the first thing we need to do is?" I asked.

"Kill all the lawyers?" replied a precocious Shakespearean scholar.

"Kill all the rules." And with that I tore up the pieces of paper.

"You can't not have no rules," said one of the boys. (*But you can not have no grammar,* I thought.)

"Rules are dumb," responded a girl. "I think we should get rid of them. They don't work anyway."

What followed was the type of spirited, intense discussion in which kids, once they know that their feelings and ideas are truly valued, rise to the highest levels of respect and responsibility extended to them. The discussion kept coming back to one central issue: If you don't have rules, how do you control behavior?

"How about this rule," I said. "'No taking things from people's cubbies.' Why was this rule made?"

"Duh," a boy replied, "because people were taking things from other people's cubbies."

"Okay. So I won't take anything out of your cubby. But it doesn't say I can't take something out of your coat pocket, or your backpack, or off your desk. Shouldn't those be rules too?"

"But you can't have a rule for everything," protested a kid.

"That's the point," said another. "If you make a hundred rules, pretty soon you need another hundred. And another."

"It's really just one rule," said a girl whose wisdom was to benefit the school many times over the next few years. "Don't do anything that harms the rights, property, or feelings of others. And I don't see why we need that as a rule. I mean," she said, looking around the room, "is there really anybody here who doesn't know that?"

"I don't," piped up a boy whose humor was to annoy the school many times over the next few years.

"But if you don't have rules," pressed another student, "how do you know what you can and can't do?"

"You know. If you just think," the girl replied.

Exactly. Rules keep children from thinking for themselves. Rules externalize children's standards for behavior. Rules teach kids to search for the letter, rather than the spirit, of the law. This leads to game-playing:

"I thought I told you not to throw balls against the house!" yells a distraught parent to her twelve-year-old.

"I'm not throwing balls against the house," responds the child indignantly. "I'm *kicking* them."

In rules-driven households, children get the message that they're not responsible for behavior that isn't explicitly prohibited.

This is the "but-you-never-said-I-*couldn't*" defense. These children also tend to believe that rules exist *because somebody says so,* rather than because the ideas contained in the rules makes sense.

"All right," said a young recovering mother when we were arguing about this issue. "I can see what you're saying. Especially for older kids. But for young children you have to have rules."

"I agree," I said. "For a short period of time, when your child is a toddler and her mobility exceeds her understanding, you need to enforce certain rules for her safety."

However, these rules—no touching the electrical sockets, no going into the street—should be considered temporary. They are cognitive training wheels, to be removed as soon as possible. Otherwise, your child learns to rely on the rules to guide her behavior rather than on her own common sense and consideration for others. Ultimately, you want your child to understand that she is not to run into the street (or the freeway, avenue, boulevard, or parking lot) not because there's a rule against it, but because it is dangerous.

Unfortunately, what happens in many households as the child matures is that the number of rules increases rather than diminishes. The child's growing independence leads to new parental policy statements regarding curfews, bedrooms, bedtimes, friends, clothing, homework, dating, telephone, food, driving, sex, drugs, drinking, and so on. Rarely is the child included in the process of establishing rules. Discipline is founded on negativity: These are the bad things that will happen if you break the rules. Discipline, however, should be motivated positively: These are the good things that will happen if you are responsible and trustworthy. What are some of these good things? Self-respect and the respect of others. Freedoms and privileges beyond what is usual for your age. Rewarding relationships with friends and family.

As an outgrowth of the discussion of rules I mentioned earlier, the children in my school invented a positively motivated system of discipline for themselves. They called it the Freesponsibility System (Freedom + Responsibility = Freesponsibility).

The system was entirely student-run. A "Freesponsibility Board" of five students and two teachers was elected by the entire student body every four weeks. It was the board's job to assign one of six "freesponsibility ratings" to students based on their demonstrated attitudes and behaviors. The higher the rating, the greater the student's autonomy and privileges. Many students quickly rose to be "5's" and "6's" and remained at that level for the years they spent at the school. It was a marvel to watch the sensitivity and creativity with which kids administered the system. Students could appeal their ratings, but the ratings were so fair that such appeals were very rare. The efforts of students to behave responsibly in order to increase their freedom were palpable. The entire school rejoiced when students who had dwelt at the lower end of the scale moved upward.

The system may sound a bit cumbersome on paper, but in practice it worked beautifully. It was simple. It taught kids that individual actions can affect the entire school community. It motivated students to their best behavior and judgment. It made them want to help their friends gain trust. It made them think about many of the issues teachers have to deal with on a daily basis. The system worked because it was designed to reward positive behavior rather than punish negative behavior. It replaced rules with reason.

When I speak of households without rules, most parents think I'm crazy. They picture a pair of helpless parents tied up in the living room while a pack of rabid teenagers destroys the house, empties the liquor cabinet, and charges admission for orgies. Certainly, this scenario is possible if parents are permissive (although I still don't think kids would charge for an orgy). The important idea to keep in mind is that *an absence of rules doesn't mean an absence of limits.*

One-day-at-a-time parents do set limits. But they do it with their child, not *to* their child. The distinction is critical.

With means we have a mutual interest in respecting each other's rights and feelings; we want each other to stay healthy and alive; we want to communicate openly and honestly; we want to grow as a family and as individuals.

To means I, the parent, am in charge; I'm not interested in your feelings and opinions; I set the rules.

With one-day-at-a-time parents it is the example they set, rather than the rules they impose, that maintains discipline. They motivate their kids to their best behavior with trust, acceptance, and a willingness to listen and share. They encourage their children to make their own decisions. They live according to the values they espouse. Isn't this what our sponsors did for us? And didn't it bring out our best?

Most of us, if every law in the world were suddenly abolished, would still want to live according to values that respect the rights, feelings, and property of others. Doing so requires not a list of rules, but empathy, good judgment, consideration, and responsibility.

What it comes down to is this: Rules don't prevent a child's "bad" behavior. Self-control does. And how does self-control develop? By helping the child to anticipate, understand, and, when necessary, experience the consequences of his actions in a safe, nonjudgmental environment.

Making Amends versus Being Punished

One of the most difficult issues for parents in recovery is knowing when and how to respond to their child's wrongdoing. The parental reflex says: *If a child does something bad, he must be punished. This is how children learn.*

True. This is how children learn. But what they learn is not how to exercise better judgment or to be more responsible, but how to be craftier and avoid detection. When parents punish, they play God. With one decree they banish their child to his room, ground him, or dock his allowance. This approach to discipline is based on threats and revenge: *If you do something bad, I'm going to do something bad to you.*

Punishments hurt and humiliate children. Often the child who is punished doesn't understand *why* he is being punished—and if he asks, it is seen as a further sign of disrespect: "You know full well why you're being punished!" Furthermore, punishments usually bear little relationship to the child's "crime." For example, what is the connection between biting a sibling and not being able to watch TV? Between not doing chores and being grounded? The perceived irrelevance and unfairness of the punishment can goad the child to further rebellion.

Punishments are based on inequality. If punishments work, it is because the parent holds the emotional, practical, and physical power cards. The child is afraid of the parent. There's a word for people who take advantage of their size to inspire fear in little kids: bullies. When fear is a cornerstone of the parent-child relationship, it sets the stage for a showdown. Sooner or later the child is going to hit back or disobey an order. Since "being sent to bed without dessert" is no longer an effective deterrent to, say, taking the car without permission, the parent needs to escalate the severity of the punishment. An arms war is set in motion: escalating punishments, escalating defiance.

The plain fact is that punishments don't work. One look at our penal system is proof of that. Soaring crime and recidivism rates suggest that the fear and fact of being punished are not effective deterrents. And, paradoxically, the people who would be deterred are generally people whose own moral code would prevent them from committing the "crime" in the first place, regardless of whether they would be punished for it. Such is the case with children too.

Punishments are similar to rules in that they both teach children to look outside of themselves for the control of behavior. What we want as parents is for our children to look inside themselves. We want our kids to say: *I'm not going to hit my brother because that will hurt him and it's not good to hurt people,* rather than: *I'm not going to hit my brother because if I do Mom won't let me go to the sleepover tonight.*

Fortunately, there is another approach to discipline. This approach encourages children to take responsibility for their actions by allowing them to experience the "logical consequences" that result. This method encourages children to think about their behavior in terms of its moral content, its practical ramifications, and its effects on themselves and others—rather than in terms of whether they'll get into trouble or not.

By focusing on making amends, we treat the child with respect. This fosters respectable behavior. The following chart shows how logical consequences differ from punishments.

Crime and Punishment
(and Logical Consequences)

The Child's Crime	A Punishment vs	A Logical Consequence
Hits his little brother.	Gets walloped so he'll learn it's wrong to hit anyone.	Must apologize to his brother and do something nice for him such as take him swimming or to a movie.
Kicks a hole in the wall during a temper tantrum.	No friends over for a week.	Has to repair the wall and pay for the materials himself.
Forgets to do his chores.	Can't go on a school trip.	Must come up with a reminder system that works or pay for the teenager his parents hire in his place.

At this point, the parental "But . . ." brigade often leaps into action:

"But doesn't this let the child off easy?"

"But what if there isn't a logical consequence?"

"But what if the child doesn't know how to fix what he broke?"

The important thing to keep in mind is that the purpose of a logical consequence is to teach, not punish. The parent is not saying to the child, "I'll show you!" but rather, "I'll show you how you can undo damage, repair relationships, and soothe hurt feelings." This approach to discipline encourages children to make amends for their behavior. If we look to our own experience, we find that making amends raises our self-esteem and helps us to feel better and act more responsibly in the future. The "victims" of our mistakes also benefit as we redress the practical and/or emotional harm we caused.

The substitution of amends for punishments does not let the child off easy. Kids feel the consequences of their actions in their piggy bank, in the time it takes to repair what they broke, in diminished parental trust, in fewer freedoms and options, in the embarrassment or troubled conscience they experience.

The beauty of an amends-based approach to discipline is that it minimizes parent-child power struggles. The parent is not an agent of revenge or an instrument of punishment and humiliation. Rather, the parent is the child's ally, conveying an expectation that the child *wants* to be responsible and trustworthy; that she *wants* to go through life without leaving a wake of destruction and bad feelings; that she *wants* to have freedom and privileges.

Here are a few ideas to keep in mind as you begin to practice this new approach to discipline:

Beware of Punishments Masquerading as Consequences

A logical consequence is the obvious, related, natural outcome of a child's action. For example, the logical consequence of knocking over a glass of milk would be to mop up the spill. The logical consequence of breaking an object would be to fix or replace it. A clear connection should be visible between the child's action, the consequences of that action, and the amends the child needs to make.

Sometimes such connections are not obvious. In such cases parents often make the mistake of camouflaging a punishment by calling it a logical consequence (e.g., "The logical consequence of your lying to me is that you can't go to the concert Friday night"). But punishments are like skunks; no matter how you dress 'em up, they still stink.

If you're not sure whether a given response to your child's behavior constitutes a logical consequence or a punishment, ask yourself the following questions:

- Does the response help my child to understand why what she did was irresponsible, hurtful, or wrong?
- Does the response allow my child to assume responsibility for her behavior?
- Does the response undo, repair, or compensate for damage done?
- Does the response help those who have been harmed to feel better?
- Does the response focus on how my child can prevent the behavior from being repeated in the future rather than on how she can be made to suffer for the past?

Obviously, not all of these questions apply in a given situation. For the ones that do, however, yes answers suggest that the response is a fitting logical consequence. No answers suggest a punishment masquerading as a logical consequence.

Put Your Kids in Charge

Why agonize over how to deal with your children's mistakes when they can do it for you? (And much better too!) When they've messed up, ask them what *they* think should be done. Let them suggest a consequence. Children as young as three can be guided toward amends they can make. Older youngsters bring huge measures of creativity, wisdom, and enthusiasm to problem solving. Once the element of punishment has been banished from the equation, kids see "how-I-can-do-it-better-in-the-future" as an intriguing challenge rather than a blow to their self-esteem. This positive, creative, future-focused atmosphere is what you want to foster.

Putting your kids in charge doesn't mean that you're a passive bystander, however. You are there to represent your own needs, perspective, and values; to help your child understand her behavior and its consequences; to lend your experience to the consideration of options; and to stand firm over issues of safety.

Kids who take responsibility for their actions develop self-confidence and self-control. They hone their problem-solving skills. They are more likely to stick to an agreement they helped to make than to one handed down from above.

Don't Add Insult to Injury

Some actions contain their own negative consequences. Avoid the temptation to add to the "punishment" your child has already received. For example, your child builds a wobbly skateboard ramp to impress his friends with some tricks and ends up with a bloodied leg and reputation. Do you really need to take his skateboard away for a week so he "learns to be more careful"?

If your child's actions have already brought sufficient negative consequences, don't add to them. Instead, help your child to understand what happened, why it happened, and how he can do things differently in the future. And then, give him love and encouragement to support him through his hard times.

Create a "Freesponsibility System"

Suggest to your children that they join you in building a family "Freesponsibility System." Have your kids identify privileges and freedoms they desire. Discuss the behaviors and attitudes requisite to such privileges. Talk about trust and responsibility. Set aside a time at family meetings (see chapter 18) to monitor progress and celebrate milestones. Help your kids see a direct link between their behavior and attitudes and the boundaries of their lives.

If you and your child disagree on the limits of his freedom, consider letting your child "try on" the privilege being sought for an agreed-upon period of time. This type of "trial period" is excellent for motivating responsibility. Make the parameters of the experiment crystal clear. You may want to draw up a written contract stating the freedom being extended, the expectations of all parties, the evaluation criteria, and the consequences for successful and unsuccessful outcomes. If he rises to the occasion, you're both winners: he, for getting what he wants; you, for having such a responsible kid!

8

Progress Not Perfection
Finding Our Children's Strengths

We are all familiar with perfectionism and the ways in which it burdened our lives. We had to be the perfect child, the perfect wife, the perfect boss, the perfect employee. Our appearance had to be perfect, as did our careers, cars, sex lives, and dinner parties.

Perfectionism tells us that we can't make mistakes. We can't be human. And if *we* can't be wrong, late, silly, or sloppy, neither can anyone else.

To seek perfection is grandiosity. To focus on the gap between perfection and what we have achieved is ingratitude. To expect others to live up to our standards is self-will run riot.

What a relief to learn in recovery that we do not have to be perfect, that we *cannot* be perfect. What a joy to be rid of our sense of self-importance, of the self-criticism that waged a never-ending war against our confidence. We are now free to be human—to relax, to laugh at ourselves, to fail!

What about our children? What messages do we give them?

"Can't you do any better than that?"

"We expect nothing but the best from you."

We know what perfectionism did to us. We must make sure it does not do the same to our children. Yet, too often, we treat our kids the way we treated ourselves. We do the following things:

- Focus on their flaws and failings.

- Allow zero tolerance for their mistakes.
- Place unrealistic expectations on them.
- Push them to achieve and then take their successes for granted.
- Compare them to siblings and other children.
- See our role as "criticizers" rather than "boosters."
- Are obsessive about the "right way" to do things.
- Make our love conditional on their performance.

A recovering mother spoke to me about the ways in which perfectionism influenced her parenting. "I can remember so clearly what it felt like when I had to be perfect. No matter what I did, it was never good enough. And that's exactly the message I gave to my child, the way I picked at her morning, noon, and night."

A recovering father spoke: "I was watching my son play soldiers with two of his friends. He was telling the two other boys what to do and where to stand, how to fall, that sort of thing. I could see he was getting more and more upset, until finally he threw the stick he was using as a gun at them and screamed, 'You're not doing it right! That's not how you're supposed to do it.' In that moment, I saw myself. That's what I had always said to him: 'You're not doing it right.' Six years old, and I had already turned him into a perfectionist."

Two things happen to children who are raised by perfectionistic parents:

1. They lose self-esteem because they can never measure up to the standard of perfection.
2. They internalize their parents' attitudes and become perfectionists themselves.

It is no wonder that these kids feel inadequate and learn to fear failure. This fear causes them to procrastinate, to avoid taking risks, and to withdraw from life in an effort to minimize the chances of "doing it wrong."

It is possible that your child has already assimilated many per-

fectionistic traits. You can help him to overcome them by practicing the following principles in all your parenting affairs:

Don't Try to Be a Perfect Parent

You don't have to be all things to your kids. And your kids don't
want you to be either. It's a lot easier for them if they don't have to
live with someone who aspires to be God. Recognize that you're
going to make mistakes as a parent. You'll lose your temper. You'll
embarrass your child in front of her friends. And this is great.
Why? Because it gives you an opportunity to do the following.

Model a Sane Attitude toward Fallibility

Show your child that it is okay to be wrong by admitting your own
mistakes. Apologize. Make an amend. Demonstrate that the world
needn't come to an end because you or your child made an error
and that an apology or a second try can usually undo whatever
damage was caused.

Introduce Failure as Your Child's Friend

Let's face it, when we fail, we feel lousy: disappointed, angry, frustrated, humiliated, stupid. While these feelings diminish with a
more accepting attitude toward failure, they are a natural human
response. If your child is upset in the face of failure, empathize
with her:

"That must have felt so frustrating."

"No wonder you're angry. You worked so hard."

Then, without belittling her feelings, help her to see that failure
often propels learning and growth. Try to point her in more hopeful and self-accepting directions by asking questions that relate to
the particular circumstance:

"Do you think you could try again?"

"It didn't work this time, but maybe there's a clue in there for next time. What do you think it is?"

Keep a List of "Goofs" in a Family Logbook

A three-ring notebook makes a good logbook. Use it to record your family's activities, goals, policies, schedules, responsibilities, and dreams; to share jokes and photos, ideas and articles; to explore feelings, structure tasks, and monitor growth. We'll refer to ways in which this can be done throughout this book.

To keep a "goof list," write the heading "A Mistake I Made Today" on the left-hand side of a page. On the right-hand side write "What I Learned from It." Encourage your kids to enter their goofs. Share your own. Some of these will be serious; others will be trivial. The cardinal rule is that no put-downs of the mistake maker are allowed.

There are many benefits to keeping a goof list: You'll stay in touch with each other's ups and downs; you'll see the humor in many mistakes; you'll encourage each other to mine mistakes for the lessons they teach.

Discuss the Concept of Perfection

Older children in particular may enjoy a meandering, philosophical discussion of perfection. The following questions can be good openers:

- Do you think perfection exists? Can you prove it?
- What types of things, if any, can truly be considered perfect? A sunset? A soufflé? An exam paper? God?

Present provocative statements for your child to debate: *There is no such thing as perfection; only unimportant things can be perfect;* and so on.

Considerations such as these will lead your child to understand the subjectivity of perfection.

Encourage Your Child to Be Wary of "Rightness"

There's a right way and a wrong way to do everything. Do you remember hearing this as a child? Much of our perfectionism was based on always having to be "right." When you think about it, though, there are very few definitively right and wrong ways to do something. When they can be found, they usually involve highly skilled, delicate operations: the right way to land an airplane, defuse a bomb, or perform open-heart surgery. What, however, is the right way to make a Caesar salad? Propose marriage? Make love?

From an early age children are straitjacketed by the adult world's obsession with being right. Nowhere are the consequences of this more damaging than in school, where the measure of learning is defined as the number of right and wrong answers a child gets on a test. The pursuit of knowledge and invention requires intellectual risk taking. What motivation does a child have to do this in a system that only values True, False, and None of the Above? No wonder studies show that schooling destroys creativity.

Even moral absolutes are not so easy to define. Of course children should be taught right from wrong. But is it as simple as that? For example, we tell children:

"It is wrong to hit."

But what if they say:

"You mean I can't hit a bully if he's kicking Timmy?"

And we say:

"It is wrong to lie."

But what if they ask:

"Won't telling the truth hurt her feelings?"

The way you live in recovery demonstrates for your child a highly moral approach to life and relationships. Within this framework of values encourage your child to find her own definitions for *right* and *wrong*. When she has to confront a moral dilemma or make a difficult choice, help her by asking questions appropriate to the situation:

"What would be the right thing to do?"
"What will happen if you do that?"
"What will happen if you don't do that?"
"What do you think the most important factors are?"

Considering the consequences of an action is often the best way for your child to assess what is "right" for her. And remember, what is right for her may be different from what is right for you.

Avoid Perfectionistic Judgments

When instructing your child to do something, acknowledge the subjectivity of right and wrong by saying:
"Let me show you how I learned to do it."
"Let me show you what I think is the easiest way."

Your child will be much more likely to accept your direction and suggestions if she is not made to feel defensive. This nonjudgmental approach not only immunizes children against perfection seeking, but encourages creativity and tolerance.

Avoid Perfectionism Masking as Encouragement

"I don't care how you do as long as you try your hardest."
"The important thing is that you do your best."

Virtually all parents make statements such as these to buck up their youngsters in the face of a challenge. Such statements are so much a part of the Parent's Lexicon that we accept them without question. And certainly, in some situations, these well-intentioned phrases do provide the child with a sense of parental love and support, as well as the important perspective that "winning isn't everything."

With the tiniest of twists, however, these exhortations go from being words of support to being demands for perfection:
"You must always try your hardest."

"If it's worth doing, it's worth doing well."

Implicit in these statements is this: *You must, at all times, in all things, do your best.* Thus, the parent, while assuring the child that perfection in *accomplishment* is not required, says that perfection in *effort* is!

Why should a child always have to try his hardest, particularly when so many of a child's challenges are not of his own choosing? Aren't there times when parents should tell their children:

"Just go out there and have fun."

"Just do as much as you have to do to satisfy the requirement."

This type of encouragement lifts the burden of perfection from a child. It allows him to allocate his resources—to strive for excellence when it matters and to be "merely" responsible or satisfactory when it doesn't.

Avoid Being a Picky Parent

Fault finding is the stock-in-trade of perfectionistic parents. The following scenes demonstrate this myopic focus at work:

Your child spends all day cutting the lawn. He comes out of the garage after putting the lawn mower away.

"You missed a spot."

Your child prances downstairs proudly after spending all afternoon getting ready for the school dance.

"Your tie is crooked."

Your child plays her new piece on the violin for you.

"I can see that *that's* going to take a lot of practicing."

How demoralizing for the child! Imagine if Charles Lindbergh, upon completing his triumphant transatlantic flight, had been greeted by the French with: "You're late!"

Try, instead, to see what was accomplished rather than what was not. The child who missed a spot on the lawn was actually diligent and responsible. The child with a crooked tie took pride in his appearance and is growing as a social being. The young violinist has passion and discipline.

A positive, encouraging approach doesn't mean you need to be blind to your child's mistakes and "minuses." But you should place your concerns in a loving, supportive context. If your child brings you a report card with five A's and a C-, focus on the good:

"Five A's! You must feel great about that. I know how hard you've been working!" Then, without accusations, without judgments, ask your child about the science grade. "I see you didn't do quite so well in science. Is that subject giving you some trouble?" This approach invites a response, not a defense.

There are a number of questions parents can ask themselves to evaluate when, whether, and how to offer their child "constructive criticism":

1. Is criticism even necessary?
   Does my child already know his error? Has he already learned from his mistake? What purpose would be served by pointing it out to him?

2. Has my child done something objectively wrong?
   Am I playing God? Is my criticism warranted on an objective level or am I simply imposing my own preferences or definitions of "rightness" upon my child?

3. How would I feel if my boss, spouse, or friends said to me the kinds of things I say to my child?

When you speak to your child, hear your words as if they were being said to you. How do they make you feel? Let that be your guide.

When parents work on their perfectionism, they work on many character defects at the same time. They work on ingratitude, compulsiveness, and the need to control. They show their child that it is okay to make mistakes, to be human. It is out of such attitudes that a child's self-confidence and desire for excellence emerge.

9

Stinkin' Thinkin'
Changing Our Feelings
by Changing Our Thoughts

Stinkin' thinkin' is the fastest route to relapse:

"Just one drink can't hurt."

"Maybe other people need to work the Steps, but not me."

"If everybody would just get off my case!"

Stinkin' thinkin' is rewriting the past. Making excuses. Playing the victim. It is self-pity, arrogance, and complacency. When we blame, whine, and rationalize, that's stinkin' thinkin'. When we figure we're better than everyone else — or worse than everyone else — that's stinkin' thinkin'.

Stinkin' thinkin' not only threatens our recovery, but poses great dangers to us as parents. This is because stinkin' thinkin' creates expectations for ourselves and our children that can never be met. We build endless lists of *shoulds* and *musts* and, when we don't get what we want, when our "needs" collide with reality, when our children don't do what they're "supposed" to, we become angry, resentful, self-damning, and depressed. In recovery, we learn that our thoughts get us into a lot of trouble and that we have to change our way of thinking. We learn that the ideas and beliefs we hold can point us toward our next drink or away from it, toward healthy relationships or away from them.

The knowledge that we can control our thinking and, in so doing, influence our emotions and behavior is one of the most valuable tools we have for maintaining sobriety and serenity. The simple idea that feelings are caused more by our thoughts about life than by life itself lies at the heart of a method of psychotherapy known as Rational-Emotive Therapy (RET).

An understanding of RET is of immense value to parents in recovery for two reasons:

1. RET provides a wonderful set of concepts and tools for meeting the challenges of child rearing.
2. RET is in perfect harmony with the principles of Twelve Step programs.

The roots of Rational-Emotive Therapy can be traced to the Stoic philosophers of the first century A.D. In *The Enchiridion* (a philosophical tome found in most dentists' waiting rooms at the time), Epictetus articulated what has become the central premise behind RET: "Men are not disturbed by things, but by the view which they take of them." Shakespeare seconded this observation when he wrote in *Hamlet:* "There's nothing either good or bad but thinking makes it so."

In the 1950s clinical psychologist Albert Ellis became disillusioned with classical psychoanalysis when he realized that his clients rarely achieved long-lasting benefits from the insights they gained. In pondering this, Ellis noted that all people held theories (ideas, beliefs, expectations) about themselves and the world. He observed that these theories—these patterns of thinking—affected and controlled the way people felt and behaved. He further observed that emotional disturbance and dysfunction in life were closely associated with highly negative self-evaluations and rigid, irrational beliefs.

The Five Premises of RET

With these discoveries in mind, Ellis founded and developed Rational-Emotive Therapy. Its theoretical underpinnings and therapeutic effectiveness have been supported by hundreds of articles and experimental studies. Rational-Emotive Therapy rests on a number of simple premises about human behavior and personality that relate directly to recovery and child rearing:

Feelings Are Caused More by How We Think about Events Than by the Events Themselves

This, the central proposition of RET, is summed up in Ellis's well-known A-B-C theory, which posits that it is not the Activating events (A) of people's lives that cause emotional Consequences (C) but rather the Beliefs (B) they hold about these events.

This goes against the grain of what we were taught as children. We grew up believing that feelings were the result of what happened to us; that is, we felt good or bad based on events, on what people said or did. A teacher keeping us after school *made* us feel angry; a parent praising us *made* us feel proud.

Since feelings were the result of external events, we reasoned that the only way we could manage our feelings would be to control the world. We tried this when we were using and discovered that it didn't work. In recovery, we learn that the only control we have is over ourselves.

The following example illustrates how your thoughts about an event can affect your emotions and behavior as a parent:

> *Your sixteen-year-old daughter begs you to lend her the car so she can drive her friends to the mall. You say okay, but that she has to have the car back by 4:00 P.M. sharp so you can go to a doctor's appointment at 5:00. It is now 4:30, and she has not returned.*

What do you feel? It all depends on what you *think*. If you think your daughter has been irresponsible and forgetful, if you think, *She shouldn't do this to me! I can't stand being kept waiting! It's going to be awful if I'm late,* you'll feel impatient, exasperated, furious.

If you believe your daughter has had an accident, if you think,

I shouldn't have given her the car. If anything ever happened to her, I couldn't live with myself, you'll feel panic, guilt, despair, helplessness.

If you believe that the car broke down or that your daughter's caught in a traffic jam, you'll have yet another set of feelings.

The various thoughts and emotions sketched in this example could lead you to any number of actions: calling a cab, notifying the police, having your daughter paged at the mall, and so on.

With this example in mind, let's examine some of the other premises upon which RET is based.

Humans Think, Feel, and Behave Simultaneously

We tend to conceive of thinking, feeling, and behaving as disparate processes. From the above example, however, we can see that this is not the case. Feelings, thoughts, and actions overlap and influence one another. Because these three processes are all part of an ongoing cycle, substantial change in one is likely to trigger substantial change in the others.

This premise is reflected in several recovery slogans: *Lead with your head and the heart will follow. Fake it till you make it. Act as if.*

Irrational Thinking Is Encouraged by Social Institutions Such as the Family, Organized Religion, and the Media

Our upbringing and culture rapidly push us into irrational thought and behavior patterns. Many religions lay down rigid absolutes of judgment and intolerance that lead to the damning of self and others; they paint virtue and sin in either-or extremes; they exhort believers toward conduct and thought that fly in the face of human nature. The resultant internal conflict ensures continual (irrational) feelings of guilt and shame.

The media condition us to expect instant solutions, instant success, and instant rewards. If we don't solve our problems in thirty minutes as people on television do, we're dysfunctional. If we don't have a million bucks, a perfect body, and a swanky apartment by the time we're twenty-five, we're worthless failures.

Families pass on their own traditions of irrational thinking when they rule that boys should not cry, that children must always be neat and obedient, that hard knocks are the best preparation for life. Children internalize these beliefs as hard-and-fast rules such as *I must always hide my feelings; if I do something bad, I am a bad person.*

Once we have these irrational beliefs, all the elements are in place for driving ourselves crazy. The next RET premise shows how we do it.

"Musturbation" Is the Cause of Most Emotional Disturbance

When we "musturbate," we take what are in reality desires—for love, money, success, approval, competence, pleasure—and turn them into absolute needs. We then view not having these "needs" met as the worst calamity that could possibly befall us.

This demandingness, Ellis theorizes, is the core of all emotional disturbance. There are four major types of demandingness:

1. I *must* do well.
2. I *must* be approved.
3. You *must* do right by me.
4. The conditions of the world *must* be fair and easy.

These *musts*, which are the very *musts* that propelled our addictions, are irrational for several reasons. First, they confuse desirability with necessity. Second, they paint the world, which is composed of many shades of gray, as black and white ("Either I am perfect or I am worthless"; "Either the world operates according to my plan or life is unbearable"). The third reason for the irrationality of demandingness is its grandiosity. To say "I *must* have" is to say "I am special—I should be spared the hardships and disappointments that life inflicts on us all."

Irrational wanting, in and of itself, doesn't lead to emotional disturbance unless the consequences of not getting what we want are defined as unendurable. This is what we do when we *awfulize.*

But awfulizing is just as irrational as demandingness. Things we consider too awful to bear—being lonely, getting fired, flunking a test—are really not awful at all when placed on the continuum of possible human suffering. Things so awful we could never stand them—losing a boyfriend, being passed over for a promotion, the bank foreclosing on our house—are, in actuality, things that we and others do "stand" every day (although there may be considerable pain and discomfort in doing so). We also find that the phoenix of future joy often rises out of the ashes of "awfulness."

By holding irrational demands and exaggerating the consequences of their being unmet, we guarantee for ourselves endless worry about getting what we want, endless worry about not getting what we want, and endless worry about keeping what we get if we actually get what we want. We guarantee that we can never live in today because the future holds the key to whether our "needs" will be fulfilled, thwarted, or threatened. We conclude that because we cannot fulfill our (irrational) needs, we are worthless, terrible human beings and end up condemning ourselves, others, and the world.

If this cycle of stinkin' thinkin' ended here, things would already be bad enough. But it gets worse. This is because of another central tenet of RET:

People Exacerbate Their Own Emotional Problems

When we are upset (or, as RET theorists would say, when we upset ourselves!), we usually know it. Since we know that it isn't "good" to feel this way, we become upset that we are upset. Now we have turned our original emotional state (being upset) into a *new*, activating event (being upset about being upset), which, according to our belief that it is terrible to be upset, makes us feel even more upset! We then whirl deeper and deeper into the vortex of our self-induced emotional hell until we have compounded our upsetment a thousandfold.

The RET approach to eradicating what Ellis calls "crooked thinking" resonates with Twelve Step tools:

> *RET is . . . designed to enable people to observe, understand, and persistently attack their irrational, grandiose, perfectionistic shoulds, oughts, and musts . . . and to . . . practice the philosophy of desiring rather than demanding and of working at changing what they can change and gracefully putting up with what they cannot.*[5]

Isn't this precisely what we learn to do in recovery? Isn't this what the Serenity Prayer is all about?

When you consider the similarities between the tenets of RET and the tools of recovery, it is not surprising that many program sayings turn out to be perfect antidotes to the kind of irrational thinking that leads to emotional disturbance and addiction:

Irrational "Stinkin' Thinkin'"	Rational "Healthy Thinking"
Nothing will ever change.	This Too Shall Pass.
People must do what I want.	Live and Let Live.
I can't stand it! I'm going to have a nervous breakdown!	Easy Does It.
I have to do my very best or I'm a terrible, rotten person.	Progress Not Perfection.
I know things aren't going to work out and it'll be awful and I won't be able to stand it.	One Day at a Time.

We all have these kinds of irrational thoughts from time to time. In recovery, we work hard to recognize and rid ourselves of them. We also need to identify the specific ways in which stinkin' thinkin' pollutes our parenting. The following are typical of the beliefs that keep us in perpetual conflict with our children and reality:

I must be a perfect parent.
I must always be loved and respected by my child.
I must always feel loving toward my child.
I must point out all my child's mistakes.

My children must do what I tell them.
My children must not get angry with me.
My children must make me proud.
My children should see things the way I do.

Beliefs such as these propel such parental pronouncements as "Don't you dare get angry with me"; "You'll think the way I tell you to think"; "If that's how you feel, you're being ridiculous."

Obviously, some of these beliefs are reasonable *preferences* for parents to hold. Others are preposterously unrealistic expectations. In either case, when we turn desires into demands and then awfulize the consequences if they are unmet, we sabotage our ability to be good parents.

Fortunately, there are a number of things we can do to root out the stinkin' thinkin' that leads to conflict and unnecessary emotional upsetment.

Take a Stinkin' Thinkin' Inventory

Before problems arise, take an inventory to seek out irrational attitudes that may be influencing your parenting behavior. If you have ongoing frustrations or conflicts with your children, try to ferret out the *shoulds* and *musts* you bring to the table. Look for instances in which you awfulize consequences. Use character defects (perfectionism, self-pity, controllingness, and so on) as lenses for sharpening your vision.

Listen for echoes of *your* parents' rules and expectations.

Chances are, whatever you heard in the past you're telling yourself (and your child) in the present.

Root Out Irrational Thinking

You can use Ellis's A-B-C model to challenge the stinkin' thinkin' that harms your effectiveness as a parent. The process is simple. Here are the steps to take when you are upset:

1. Identify the emotional consequences (C) (i.e., how you feel).
2. Identify the activating event (A) that triggered these feelings.
3. List your beliefs (B) about the event and its emotional consequences.
4. Dispute (D) your stinkin' thinkin'.
5. Engage (E) rational thoughts.
6. Formulate (F) new goals and a plan of action.

In order to understand how this works, let's approach a typical parent-child conflict in two different ways. The first scenario shows the effects of unchecked stinkin' thinkin'.

> *You come home from work, hot, tired, and in a terrible mood after rush-hour traffic. You pull into the garage to find a disaster area: overflowing garbage cans, bikes, toys, tools strewn across the floor. That morning, before leaving the house, you had told your thirteen-year-old son to clean up the garage.*
>
> Damn that kid, *you think.* What is wrong with him? I CAN'T STAND being ignored like this. *You're so angry, you kick one of the garbage cans. Trash flies all over the place. A can of oil spills on the floor, drenching your shoe.* Now look what he's done! He MADE me so angry, he's ruined my shoes. The garage MUST be cleaned up immediately.

In my house people MUST do what I say. He is going to HAVE TO BE punished for this.

You storm into the house and burst into your son's room. Your startled son and two of his friends look up. "When I tell you to do something, I expect to be obeyed. Do you understand? I want that garage cleaned up NOW! Do you hear me? NOW!"

Your son and his companions troop out of the room in embarrassed silence. The friends go home. Your son works into the night. You've cooled down some and you begin to think: Boy, I really lit into him something fierce. And in front of his friends too. He must feel AWFUL. It's TERRIBLE that I get so angry. I'm a HORRIBLE parent!

In this scenario, stinkin' thinkin' powers the interaction. The father's demandingness that things SHOULD and MUST be a certain way, and that it is AWFUL when they are not, ignites his rage. At the end of the evening, the scorecard looks like this:

One father feeling a residue of fury, guilt, and shame.
One son feeling angry, humiliated, and confused.
One problem unexplored, unresolved, and bound to recur.

Not a very productive approach. Now let's play back the identical scenario, responding to it the way a one-day-at-a-time parent would. Let's use the tools of RET to root out the stinkin' thinkin'.

You come home from work in a terrible mood and find that the garage is a disaster. You're so angry, you— STOP in your tracks! You count to ten. In that time you remember that emotional upsetment is usually caused by stinkin' thinkin'. You decide to use the A-B-C approach before confronting your son. You get out a piece of paper and write

1. Feelings (C)
2. Activating Event (A)
3. Beliefs (B)   4. Dispute Irrational   5. Engage Rational
                           Thoughts (D)   Thoughts (E)
6. Formulate Goals and Plan (F)

Now you're ready to go to work.

1. Identify the emotional consequences (C) of this event. How do you feel? Listen to your gut, not your head. Avoid interpretations masked as pseudofeelings *(I feel that I'm a failure; I feel I shouldn't get so mad)*. You write

   I feel angry. Frustrated. Disappointed. Resentful.

2. Identify the activating event (A) that triggered these feelings. Be as objective and factual as you can. Remember that thoughts and feelings can also be activating events. You write:

   I asked my son to clean the garage.
   I come home and saw that the garage was still a mess.
   I flew into an internal rage.
   I felt I was a failure as a parent.

3. List your beliefs (B) about the event and its emotional consequences.

   Write down all the thoughts going on in your head. Don't forget any thoughts you have about your feelings.

4. Dispute (D) your stinkin' thinkin'.
   Do battle with your *shoulds, musts,* and *awfuls.* Ask yourself: *Who says? Show me the rule. What is the evidence?*

5. Engage (E) rational thoughts.
   Replace every irrational thought generated in step three with a rational one. Your RET worksheet might look something like this:

3. Beliefs (B)	4. Dispute Irrational Thoughts (D)	5. Engage Rational Thoughts (E)
My son MUST always be responsible.	Why MUST he always be responsible? Am I? Do I even know that irresponsibility was the cause of what happened?	I'd like my son to always be responsible but it's not a realistic expectation to have for a child.
The garage MUST be kept clean.	Is this a law I have seen? Why does a garage HAVE TO be clean?	I PREFER having a clean garage. Others may not share this preference.
I CAN'T STAND being ignored like this.	How do I know I WAS ignored? This is an assumption. There may be some other explanation. And I AM standing it.	I PREFER not to be ignored when I make a request. Perhaps some problem occurred in communication.
My son has MADE me so angry!	My son is nowhere to be seen. I have made myself angry by defining my desires as demands that must be met or else!	I have a CHOICE about how I feel. My thoughts control to a large extent whether I get upset or not.
The garage MUST be cleaned immediately.	Why immediately? What difference does it make whether it is cleaned immediately or tomorrow or this weekend?	I would PREFER that the garage be cleaned as soon as possible. In reality, it makes no difference to my life over the next few days.

3. Beliefs (B)	4. Dispute Irrational Thoughts (D)	5. Engage Rational Thoughts (E)
My son has done something TERRIBLE and must be punished.	Killing a schoolmate is TERRIBLE. Setting fire to the house is TERRIBLE. But not cleaning the garage? Puh-lease!	MAYBE my son has been forgetful and irresponsible. I don't know that for sure. I need to talk to him to see what the problem is and how we can solve it.
I'm a HORRIBLE parent for losing my temper.	What proof do I have for this judgment? What about all my good qualities? Is there any evidence that I'm abusive and unloving?	Nobody's perfect. Just because I lost control on this occasion doesn't mean I'm not a good parent. I can make an effort to deal with my anger better.

You are now prepared for the final step of the RET approach:

6. Formulate (F) new goals and a plan of action.
Write down what you would like to see happen and how you plan to achieve your goals. (You can incorporate problem-solving techniques such as those discussed in chapter 18.) For example:

Goals:

1. *Find out why the garage wasn't cleaned up.*
2. *Prevent similar breakdowns of responsibility and/or communication from recurring.*
3. *Arrive at a mutual understanding with my son about his chores and household responsibilities.*
4. *Get the garage clean.*
5. *Control my temper.*

Plans to achieve goals:

> 1. *Talk to my son to find out what happened and how we can prevent it from happening in the future.*
> 2. *Tell my son how I feel when I see the garage in such a state.*
> 3. *Put "How to keep the garage clean" on a family meeting agenda.*
> 4. *Count to ten. Meditate. Use the RET steps to keep better control of my emotions.*

Having exposed the stinkin' thinkin' that stoked your furnace, you've cooled down enough to see the incident in perspective. You feel annoyed but not enraged. Disappointed but not depressed. You also realize that you have an incomplete understanding of the event. Perhaps your son thought he had a few days in which to do the job; perhaps your spouse commandeered him for another task. Under the American system of justice, your son is innocent until proven guilty.

At this point, you are mentally and emotionally prepared to go to your son and say, "I noticed that the garage is still a mess." You don't say, "I thought I told you to clean up the garage" or "Do you think you can just ignore me when I ask you to do something?"

You want to state a fact, not make an accusation. This way no one's on the defensive. Once you understand what happened, you'll know the issues you need to discuss. You will have the entire repertoire of one-day-at-a-time parenting tools at your disposal: family meetings, problem-solving sessions, reflective listening, positive communication techniques, and so on.

Encourage Children to Think Rationally

Earlier I described some of the ways in which culture and upbringing foster stinkin' thinkin'. It is likely that your children have already internalized many irrational beliefs. Some of these they got from growing up in an alcoholic home (*I must be a BAD, ROT-*

TEN kid or otherwise my mother wouldn't drink; I MUST be PER-FECT). Other irrational beliefs they learned in school and from the barrage of cultural messages with which they have been assaulted since birth *(It's AWFUL to be unpopular; If I don't lose ten pounds I'm a TOTAL FAILURE).*

You can help your children to recognize and dispute their own irrational beliefs in a number of ways:

Set an Example of Rational Thinking

Children pick up on their parents' attitudes and thoughts. Be alert to the messages you give your children. You teach them that feelings come from the outside when you say:
"You kids are driving me crazy!"
"You're making Daddy very angry!"

You teach your children to awfulize when you tell them:
"If you don't stop fighting, I'm going to lose my mind!"
"I can't stand it when you talk with your mouth full."

You teach your kids to think in black and white when you say:
"You always think of yourself."
"I'm never going to be able to trust you again."

Your kids will demonstrate that they've mastered these forms of stinkin' thinkin' when they begin to say things like:
"You never let me do anything."
"You always take her side."
"My teacher gets me so mad!"

"Oh come on," parents have said to me, "isn't this all a bit nitpicky? You mean to say that if I tell my child he's being *awful* or that he's *driving me crazy,* he's going to take me literally? It's just a figure of speech."

Of course, as children mature they come to understand the figurative aspects of language. They know that they don't *really* have egg on their face when embarrassed or butterflies in their stomach when nervous. Young children, however, think in very concrete terms. If a four-year-old hears that someone is "tied up at the moment," that child pictures a body bound in ropes. If kids grow up with a steady diet of *awfuls* and *terribles, musts* and *shoulds, always* and *nevers,* they will adopt the meanings and proportions with which their parents endow these words into their understanding of themselves and the world.

Thus, the first step you can take to encourage your child to think rationally is to monitor your own language. Listen for, and avoid, expressions that reflect demandingness, awfulizing, and musturbation.

Role-Play Alternative Responses to Events

A grasp of the abstractions that underlie RET requires a level of understanding that is beyond most preadolescents. This doesn't mean, however, that RET principles cannot be used to great effectiveness by younger children as a means of dealing with emotional upsetment.

You can present these concepts by encouraging your child to role-play alternative emotional and behavioral responses to events. (He can also act them out with dolls, toys, friends, and/or siblings.) Let's say your eight-year-old wants to go off with his older sister and her friends to a shopping mall. They refuse to let him come. Consequently, he yells at his sister, calls her names, and says he is going to break her fish tank. He storms to his room and slams the door—twice, just in case you didn't hear it the first time.

After giving your son some time to calm down, you go to his room. "I see that you are upset that you couldn't go with Sarah," you say. "Getting upset is one way of acting when you feel angry or disappointed." Verbalize the irrational thinking that accompanies this response: "I'm so mad. It's not FAIR. I MUST go with them. Sarah's a TERRIBLE, ROTTEN MEANIE for not letting me go. It's AWFUL that I can't go."

Ask your child to act out some other ways he might respond. If he draws a blank, you can act them out: "You could go to your room and cry. *'Waaaaah. Nobody likes me. I can never do anything I want!'* Or you could sing a happy song to cheer yourself up.

"Let's see, what else could you do? You could do a somersault and stand on your head." Note that humor is an excellent ally for helping your child to become aware of alternatives. Just be sure you don't use it to belittle your child's suggestions or current upsetment. Continue to propose and model options for behavior and emotion: "You could tell yourself: *'I know Sarah likes me. She just wanted to be with her friends the way I like to be with my friends. I could ask her to take me some other time.'* Or, you could say to yourself: *'I really wanted to go with Sarah. But being sad won't change anything. So now I'm going to think of something else to do that would be fun.'*"

Help your child to understand that emotional upsetment usually has no effect on the event that "caused" it, the perpetrator of the "injustice," or the consequences that resulted. Emotional upsetment just makes the upset person more upset.

Young children will not understand the concept of "rational" versus "irrational" thinking. They will, however, understand that some thoughts lead to temper tantrums, breaking things, hurting others, losing privileges, and feeling sad, mad, lonely, and scared whereas other thoughts lead to staying in control, keeping friends, being trusted, and feeling happy, proud, and capable. Use concepts such as these, for which your child already has reference points, to portray the distinctions between rational and irrational thinking.

Remember that these are sophisticated ideas. Don't expect your child to understand or embrace them right away. Just try to keep your child in touch with the basic concepts so that they will become second nature to her as she matures.

Helping Adolescents to Think Rationally

Unlike younger children, adolescents do possess the cognitive skills to understand the abstractions upon which RET is based.

You can talk to teenagers about rational and irrational thinking, about disputing one's belief system, about the interplay of thoughts, feelings, and behavior. There is, however, one pitfall. An astute recovering mother quickly identified it during a discussion we were having about parenting and RET:

"I keep hearing you say that we shouldn't ridicule or label our children's ideas and feelings. But isn't that exactly what I'm doing when I tell her that her thoughts are silly and irrational? Isn't that a contradiction?"

Yes, it is—if *you* are the one doing the telling. And for this reason you must not. What you want to do instead is lead your child to see the irrationality herself. You are not a Rational-Emotive Therapist. You are a parent. The therapist role permits a more confrontational stance. Such an approach requires training as well as the secure boundaries provided by the therapeutic relationship and is not an appropriate one for parents to undertake. The therapist can say: "Your thoughts are irrational and unfounded." (In other words, "You're being silly.") The parent cannot. What you can do, however, is encourage your child to come to such a conclusion on her own ("I'm really being silly, aren't I?").

The following suggestions will help you to put the principles of RET at your adolescent's disposal.

Show Your Child How Thoughts Influence Feelings

Present the following scenario:

> *Your child rides her bike to school. After school she'll be going off with some friends, which is something she's been looking forward to for weeks. When the bell rings, she goes to get her bike and it's gone. How does she feel?*

If your child says, "It depends," it means she already understands the relationship between suppositions (beliefs) and emotions. Draw her out as she considers different scenarios and how they would make her feel. If your child simply responds to your question by saying she'd feel angry because someone stole it or scared because she'd get in trouble at home, ask her:

"How would you feel if you thought your best friend had just borrowed it for a few minutes?"

"You thought a child being chased by a kidnapper had used it to get away?"

"You knew you were getting a brand-new one for your birthday?"

"You had forgotten to lock it?"

Considering an event from the perspective of different assumptions makes the connection between assumptions, beliefs, and feelings explicit for your child.

Help Your Child to Recognize Her Irrational Thoughts

Many of a child's statements contain an unspoken irrational assumption. For example:

"I hate Mr. Brown for keeping everybody after class." *(Because it's not fair and the world should be fair.)*

"You have no right to tell me I can't go." *(Because I should be able to do anything I want.)*

When your child makes statements such as these, help her to identify the thoughts behind her feelings. You can do this by prompting her with an *and* or a *because* or by asking such questions as:

"Why do you feel that way?"

"What makes you say that?"

Once an irrational belief is elicited, you'll need to show your child how to recognize and challenge it.

Help Your Child to Dispute Her Irrational Thoughts

Children's stinkin' thinkin', like that of adults, tends toward patterns of awfulizing, demanding, and self-downing.

If your child awfulizes, ask:

"Is there another way you could look at the situation so that you're not so upset?"

The child kept after school might say: "Mr. Brown didn't use a good strategy for dealing with the problem, but he's still a pretty good teacher."

Another thing you can do is ask:

"What's the worst thing that could happen?"

Encourage your child to play out the "terrible" scenario in her mind. She will see that it isn't that terrible after all.

Reflect Your Child's Irrational Statements Back to Him

Adolescents use adjectives such as *awful, terrible,* and *horrible* so frequently that they may resist the fact that the words themselves fuel their suffering. Help your adolescent recognize that the words he uses to shape his description of an event also shape his emotional response. What if, instead of it being AWFUL and HORRIBLE, it was DISAPPOINTING and UNPLEASANT? Wouldn't he feel better? Be able to cope better? Make it clear to your child that you are not challenging his right to his feelings. Rather, you're sharing some strategies you've found useful for keeping people and events from controlling you.

When your child's awfulizing takes the form of "I can't stand it!" say:

"What does it mean if a person can't stand something?"

Most adolescents will recognize that something can be a real pain in the neck and still be bearable—that, in fact, for quite some time they are, and have been, standing all kinds of things they say they can't stand. If something were truly "unstandable," it would cause them to faint, go insane, or die. If your child faces an unpleasant situation, acknowledge it, but emphasize that you know he is a strong, capable person who can stand upsetting things. A child who feels he *can* stand things will be more confident than a child who feels he can't.

Similar challenges to stinkin' thinkin' can be made when your child says: "This is IMPOSSIBLE! I'll NEVER be able to do this." These thoughts lead a child to feel defeated, angry, worthless. Say to your child: "There's NO chance at all that you can do it?" Your child will see that what she calls impossible is merely difficult. This means that, with work and perseverance, she may very well be capable of doing it.

Demandingness is another common form of stinkin' thinkin' that children practice:

"I HAVE to go!"

"I HAVE to have new sneakers."

"I MUST have a boyfriend."

You can help your child to recognize this type of irrational thought by talking about the difference between needs and wants. A "need" is something we *must* have for survival (air, water, food). A "want" is something we *would like to have* but don't have to have (popularity, boyfriends, new sneakers, love). We may feel unhappy, uncool, or uncared for if we can't have our "wants." But we won't die.

The line between accepting your child's thoughts and feelings and reflecting them in such a way that she recognizes them to be irrational is a fine one. You can minimize the possibility that your child will take your comments the wrong way if you

1. Challenge her ideas at a neutral time when you're not in the midst of a conflict.

2. Address situations in which you are not personally involved.

3. Engage your child's complicity. Ask her if she would like to learn some strategies for dealing with feelings, people, and events that can be upsetting. Most teenagers will welcome such help if it is presented with respect. Make it a project you'll work on together.

Helping Children Who Dump on Themselves

Adolescents are especially prone to self-downing thoughts. There are a number of things you can do to help them to develop and maintain a good opinion of themselves.

- Discuss what makes people "human." Try to get across some of the following ideas: People are complicated creatures; people are made of many different qualities—some of them positive, some negative; everybody makes mistakes; people are not bad because they make mistakes.

- Suggest that your child draw a big circle that is her whole self. Inside this big circle she will draw smaller ones that represent aspects of her self: traits, talents, good and bad habits, strengths, limitations, dreams, fears, and so on. This demonstrates graphically that people are made up of many different qualities. One "bad" circle doesn't take away from other "good" circles.[6]

- Children often dump on themselves when they've made a mistake. You can help your child to develop a more rational attitude toward mistakes by suggesting that she fill in the following chart:

Mistake	Cause	Thoughts about Mistake Maker	Ways Mistake Might Be Avoided in the Future
1. A baby spills milk on the new carpet.			
2. Tom crashes his father's car.	A bee stung him.		
3. Tom crashes his father's car.	Tom was drinking.		

Mistake	Cause	Thoughts about Mistake Maker	Ways Mistake Might Be Avoided in the Future
4. Sally pleaded to be sent away to camp. After one week she hated it and came home.			
5. Frank forgot to bring his homework to school.	Frank failed to set his alarm and had to rush to school.		
6. Frank forgot to bring his homework to school.	Frank ran out of the house because his parents were fighting.		

Children should be encouraged to use this exercise to consider such issues as What causes mistakes (inattention, fatigue, insensitivity, poor judgment, and so on)? What makes a mistake a mistake? Is someone always to "blame" for a mistake? How do different contexts affect the way we view our mistakes? What roles do others play in our own mistakes? What can we learn from mistakes?

- Encourage your child to dispute negative self-talk. Let him see that he can express a negative thought without condemning his character or capabilities.

Negative Self-Talk	Positive Self-Talk
Everybody hates me.	Not *everybody* hates me. Ben likes me. Mrs. Silver likes me. My parents like me. I sure would like to have more friends, though.

Negative Self-Talk	Positive Self-Talk
I can't do anything right.	I'm good at some things. Just because I wrecked my project doesn't mean I can't do anything right. I'll try to be more careful next time.
I never know what to say.	I wish I hadn't said what I said. But I don't say the wrong thing *every* time I open my mouth. Lots of times I know what to say.
I can't stand it when they tease me at school.	I sure don't like being teased. But I can live with it if I have to.

- When kids "junk" themselves, show them how to turn self-talk into pep talk. Your child can give himself the "home-team" advantage if he acts as his own cheerleader:

  Okay, just stay calm. Deep breaths. Worrying won't help. Even if you blow it, it's not the end of the world. Just take it one step at a time. Don't freak out. You don't have to prove anything. You've come through situations like this before. You can do it!

Teach Problem-Solving Skills

When children are unhappy or anxious, and their minds are running overtime with stinkin' thinkin', it's often because they don't have the skills to deal with the problems they face. You can cut down on a lot of the irrational thinking produced by worry and fear if you make sure that your child is familiar with problem-solving strategies (see chapter 18).

10

This Too Shall Pass
Allowing Our Children to Grow
According to Nature's Timetable

This too shall pass is an important cognitive tool for maintaining perspective and outlasting pain. As one-day-at-a-time parents, we use this slogan to sustain us during periods of worry and heartache. We use it to endure our children's fads and foibles; who among us has not said *This too shall pass* during our children's terrible twos or hormonal high-school days? (And who among us has not turned around a few years later to bemoan the speed with which our kids are growing!)

This too shall pass is letting things unfold at their own pace, in their own way. It is remembering that we are not the timekeepers of the universe.

Said a recovering mother of three at the end of a particularly trying day, "I think God invented children as a means of teaching patience."

Why are we so impatient with everyone and everything around us? Because we are impatient with ourselves. We were always this way—always restless, chafing, living outside of today. We couldn't wait—until dinner, until the holidays, until summer vacation, until we got a driver's license, until we were out of school, until we had a girlfriend or boyfriend, until we were rich and famous. We couldn't wait for events to take their course, for emotional pain to heal. But that was all right because we had the instant cure—Dr. Feelgood's magic elixir—in liquid, powder, or high-caloric form!

Impatience accompanied us into recovery. We wanted serenity *now*. We wanted to shed our character defects *now*. We wanted to solve our marital and family problems *now*. Many of us tried to set new land-speed records for working the Steps. And for all our impatience, did we get where we wanted to go any faster? No. We just guaranteed that the journey would be full of anxiety and frustration. We even discovered that some of the destinations we were so impatient to get to weren't on our "cruise director's" agenda.

Impatient parents can't wait until their child is out of diapers. They can't wait until she goes to nursery school. Impatient parents are always in a rush:

"Hurry up!"

"Here, let me do it."

Impatient parents misinterpret dawdling as disobedience. They yank their child along the sidewalk. They finish his sentences. They don't let him dress himself. The more they try to hurry their child's growth, the more they slow it down. If you push a child who's running, he doesn't go faster. He falls. Pushy parents set their kids up for a fall.

Nature has worked out a very lovely plan for the development of children: She only gives them as much as they can handle. When parents are impatient, they dishonor their child's natural timetable for growth.

When we are impatient, we miss the joy of today with our children. You can enhance your ability to respect the pace of your child's development if you keep the following ideas in mind.

Travel to Your Child's Time Zone

A child's sense of time is very different from an adult's. In infancy, a baby begins to distinguish between "now" and "not now." Slowly, the child develops an understanding of time as a sequence of events: *Mommy comes home; we eat dinner; I have my bath; I go to bed.* This ability to order events is an important cognitive milestone. Parents can tell that their child has mastered it when the child's actions indicate anticipation of "what's next," e.g., handing Daddy a book in advance of story time, using delaying tactics right before bedtime.

As they mature, children learn to tell time, count days, and refer to the months and seasons. Their ability to do so outpaces their understanding of the abstract concepts involved. Time is still highly personal and relative; if they are bored, ten minutes is a longer period of time than three hours spent at an amusement park. You've seen this on car trips:

"How much longer till we're there?"

"We'll be there in one hour."

Three minutes later: "Are we there yet?"

When your five-year-old dawdles and delays, she does not connect her behavior to "making you late." She assumes that the doctor will see her—that the next event will happen—when she gets there. When you say to your six-year-old, "I want you dressed and ready in ten minutes," and twenty minutes later he's still in bed, don't assume he understood what *ten minutes* meant.

You can maintain your patience and serenity in the face of such frustrations by remembering the following keep-it-simple tips:

Allow More Time

For many years a good friend of mine has been kind enough to drive me to the airport on occasion when I travel. She is a busy, efficient real estate broker who is never without a list of errands a mile long. One reason she gets so much done is that she knows how to maximize the output of any effort. Thus, a trip to the airport includes picking up a lockbox, dropping off a contract, and stopping at the bank, pharmacy, and post office. There is never any doubt in my friend's mind that we will arrive at the airport with time to spare. Her definition of *time to spare,* however, is different from mine. After a few harrowing (for me) rides, I came upon the *keep-it-simple* solution: If my plane leaves at 3:00, I tell her it leaves at 2:30. Thus, when we get to the airport at 2:15, there really is time to spare.

If your child is always "making you late," set your own watch a half hour ahead. That way you'll end up right on time.

Hide the Digital Clock

Digital clocks delay a child's understanding of time. This is because such clocks merely *count* the passage of time. They do not *show* it. Be sure you have a number of "old-fashioned" clocks around the house. "When the big hand is on the four"; "When the little hand goes all the way around"—this is how kids learn not only to tell time but to grasp the idea of it.

Relate Time to Your Child's Personal Experience

Understanding requires that we relate something new to something we already know. To say that frozen yogurt is like ice cream means nothing if we don't know what ice cream is like. Similarly, to tell a child that a birthday party is in four days tells him nothing if he doesn't have a concrete grasp of what four days is. You can facilitate such understanding by referring to time in terms of things your child knows: "We'll be there in twenty minutes. That's how long it takes to walk from our house to the park."

Remember That It Takes Time to Create Good Things

Destruction occurs quickly. A cathedral that took centuries to build can be bombed to rubble in seconds. A Rembrandt, a Stradivarius, a majestic rain forest can all be destroyed in a moment.

Children and other good things need time to grow. Allow them the weeks, months, and years it takes. Next time you're feeling impatient with your child's rate of development, instead of focusing on how long your child is taking, consider how miraculous it is that children are able to master so much so quickly.

Learn about the Developmental Stages of Children

It's easier to be patient with your child's three steps forward and two steps back if you have a basic understanding of child development. A lot of a child's growth involves preparation, becoming ready. Such growth is often invisible. Learn what's appropriate and expected at different ages. The fact that it's perfectly normal for children to hit puberty within a span of five or six years shows that nature allows considerable leeway for development. If nature is patient, you can be too.

Remember What You Were Like at This Age

When you're feeling impatient with your child, remember what it was like when you were a kid: people always telling you to get busy and stop goofing off; never enough time to do the things you wanted to do. Let your kids stop to sniff the flowers and play with the pebbles. Let them have free time. Let them lie in their beds and stare at the ceiling. After all, as a kid I know says, "If you don't daydream, you won't get anywhere in life."

Helping Children to Be Patient

It is not in the nature of most children to be patient. The ability to delay gratification develops slowly. In part this is due to a child's limited sense of time, which we discussed earlier. It is also due to two other powerful forces: human nature and society. The ability to satisfy one's needs quickly has survival value. One can delay food, shelter, and treatment of illness or injury only so long before it becomes life threatening. Thus, there is likely some evolutionary purpose served in wanting what we want when we want it.

Our culture also encourages children to demand immediate satisfaction of their desires. In this "Age of Instantaneity," stores are open twenty-four hours a day; you can even buy what you want before you have what it takes to pay for it. With faxes and express mail the pressure to get things done faster than necessary has ratcheted up yet another notch. Kids watch their television heroes solve problems in thirty minutes flat (unless the problem is a really big one, in which case sixty minutes are needed). The message kids get from this media-driven "presto-lization" is that success comes with little effort; that reward is their due; and, most damaging of all, that something is wrong with them if their life isn't as neat as a scriptwriter's vision.

One has to wonder how much teenage depression, drug use, suicide, and violence are caused by kids feeling that they aren't "stacking up" or getting what they "deserve."

Fostering patience in children is an uphill battle. But it can be done if you keep these ideas in mind.

Help Your Kids Set Realistic Goals

It's great to dream, but kids lose patience when they don't see themselves making any progress toward those dreams. Goals need to be realistic for your child's age and abilities. Children are more likely to summon the patience to persevere when they are aware of the relationship between what they are doing today and what they would like to have done by tomorrow. You can encourage this patience by showing your child how to prioritize, celebrate milestones, and break tasks down into manageable steps.

Give Your Child the Gift of This Too Shall Pass

When your kids are stuck in a situation they think will never end—a work crunch at school, a broken heart, a falling out with a friend—commiserate with their upsetment. Then suggest that they try saying *This too shall pass* to themselves. Explain that people use this expression as a way of reminding themselves that feelings and fallout will eventually lessen or go away. Ask them to remember a toothache they had, or a broken leg that kept them on crutches for six weeks, or a teacher who made school a nightmare—miseries that, at the time, seemed without end but which are now distant memories. When your child's life feels dark and gloomy, *This too shall pass* is a candle she can light until the sun comes out.

Encourage Activities That Involve the Delay of Gratification

Activities such as reading, collecting, lifting weights, learning to play a musical instrument, gardening, and cooking all reward your child for patience and perseverance. It may be the yummy cake he gets to eat, the flowers he gets to enjoy, or the muscles he gets to flex. Your child will realize that good things often come in slow-arriving packages.

Bury a Time Capsule

Decide what kind of a time capsule it's going to be and for how long you're going to bury it. Perhaps it's a "Summer Reminders" capsule to be opened in the dead of winter. Perhaps it's a "My Tenth Year" capsule to be opened on your child's twelfth birthday. Be sure to use a container that can stand up to the elements.

Model Patience

If your child is constantly chomping at the bit, if she's never content with the way things are, consider whether she may be getting her cues from you. If you slow your expectations down from Mach 3, if you stop trying to control the timetable of the universe, if you use *This too shall pass* to keep a lid on impatience, she will too.

11

Count to Ten
Understanding and Resolving Conflict
with Our Children

Better yet, count to a thousand. In fact, for really serious conflicts, count to a hundred thousand! Then go for a walk, sit by a lake, watch the sunset, and get a good night's sleep! Now you are ready to deal with the problem.

Unfortunately, most of us cannot respond to conflict in this sybaritic manner. We have to find other ways. Nothing could be more important to our personal recovery, our children, and the health of our family relationships.

If you think about it, conflict is really what our lives have been about since day one. We became experts at both seeking and fleeing it. Now we must become experts at understanding and resolving it.

First, let's get one thing said: Conflict is good. It is natural, healthy, and inevitable. It is how we grow and how we know we have outgrown. The baby chick breaking out of its shell is in conflict with it. The adolescent who wants more freedom is in conflict with the protective instincts of her parents. The young adult torn between two career paths is in conflict with himself. It is never conflict per se that causes harm. It is *unresolved* conflict that causes harm. *Improperly* resolved conflict. *Unfairly* resolved conflict—conflict that leaves people feeling hurt, ignored, manipulated, and abused.

One-day-at-a-time parents do not strive to eliminate conflict from their families. Rather, they strive to identify it and to resolve it in ways that respect the needs and feelings of everyone involved. This leads to personal growth for each family member, better communication, warmer affections, and fewer conflicts in the future.

Why is conflict between parents and children inevitable? Let me count the ways. Conflicts result from clashing needs, issues of independence and control, hurt feelings, failure to live up to expectations, unclear communication, rigid thinking, incompatible values and priorities, discordant definitions of what constitutes "responsibility," "good judgment," "consideration," "carelessness," and so on.

In the past, we probably reacted to conflicts such as these by yelling, attacking, shaming, scaring, withdrawing, sulking, playing doormat, denying, threatening, and/or manipulating.

When you examine these methods for dealing with conflict, you realize that they don't deal with it at all. Because of the power cards parents hold, they are often successful in using physical and psychological intimidation to get what they want. But these methods ultimately fail because, sooner or later, the kids call their parents' bluff. They rebel and disobey. They get too big to hit. Parents can escalate their threats and attacks, but children can escalate their defiance. Eventually, the parent-child relationship is destroyed.

Implicit in these unhealthy reactions to conflict is this: *The way to solve conflict is to get the other person to change.* If there is one thing we have learned in recovery, it is that we cannot change or control others. But we can change and control ourselves. We can choose the attitudes and feelings we wish to embrace and those we wish to reject. The only tool we have for influencing the behavior of others is our own behavior.

Dealing with Parent-Child Conflict

The attitudes you adopt can go a long way toward determining (1) how often conflict arises and (2) how effectively and peaceably it can be resolved. What are some of these attitudes?

Healthy Attitude 1. I have every reason *not* to know how to deal with conflict.

I may have grown up in a family that taught only harmful and ineffective means of problem solving. I was never offered a course at school on how to have healthy relationships or be a good parent. I look around at the world today and see countless examples of individuals, groups, and governments unable to settle their differences. I needn't cast blame upon myself, but now, recognizing my limitations in this area, I can seek to grow.

Healthy Attitude 2. I recognize that conflict is a normal, natural, and unavoidable element in all healthy families.

I will not measure the health of my relationships with my children by whether we are in conflict or not; rather, I will measure it by the degree of honesty, understanding, and respect we bring to resolving our differences. I will recognize that conflict can help us to grow closer as a family and to learn more about each other's feelings and needs.

Healthy Attitude 3. I understand that in recovery the amount of conflict in my life may initially increase.

I will let go of the unrealistic expectation I had that *everything would be all right once I stopped using.* My recovery has thrown all the old family patterns of coping and enabling up in the air. As a family, we are now searching for new roles and relationships. We are moving toward being able to feel, identify, and work on our problems for the first time. Buried issues will surface. This will create conflict. My own personal recovery makes me particularly vulnerable to *internal* conflict as I find that many of my old friendships, attitudes, and behaviors are no longer possible or desirable.

Healthy Attitude 4. I recognize that conflict represents not only disagreement but caring.

Our grappling means that we haven't given up. We still care— otherwise we wouldn't fight so much! This gives us something to build upon.

Healthy Attitude 5. I will not try to win arguments. I will try to solve problems.

My role as parent does not automatically entitle me to supremacy over my child's needs and feelings. Our goal as a family is to find solutions that work for everybody, not just somebody.

Healthy Attitude 6. I will stop thinking in terms of either-or, black and white.

Many seemingly insoluble standoffs can be brought to swift resolution if I am willing to hear and accept other viewpoints as valid. Compromise is often the fastest route to getting what I want and need.

Healthy Attitude 7. I can ask for help.

I do not have to assume all the responsibility for solving family problems. I can ask for help from my spouse, children, friends, or Higher Power.

Healthy Attitude 8. Not all conflict can be resolved to my total satisfaction.

I will not approach problem solving with my old expectations of perfection. We are human beings, not machines. On those occasions when we cannot work through our pain or conflict, I will do everything I can to accept it and ensure that the lack of resolution does not harm my children or me. I will remember that my children have the right to differ with me and that our differences do not mean we love one another less.

CARE

Now that you are basking in all these healthy attitudes, you probably can't wait to get your hands on a conflict. Don't worry. It'll come soon enough! And when it does, you'll know what to do if you remember four steps, the first letters of which, by an amazing lexical coincidence, spell the word *CARE*:

1. **C**ount to ten
2. **A**sk questions
3. **R**eflect
4. **E**ngage

Keep in mind that these four steps form a fluid, interactive process. But, in the same way that learning to swim is easier if it is broken down into separate elements—floating, breathing, kicking—so, too, is learning to resolve conflict. With this in mind, let's take a closer look at how you CARE.

Step 1: Count to Ten

When conflict arises, the immediate danger is that it will flare out of control. Emotions will overrun rational thought. This is when hateful and hurtful remarks are made, when objects are thrown, when physical abuse occurs.

Counting to ten provides immediate damage control. Take deep breaths. Shake your limbs. Meditate. Go outside for some air.

Obviously, it is not always possible to absent yourself from a conflict. Many issues must be dealt with in the moment. But it is a rare conflict indeed that doesn't allow you ten seconds in which to take deep breaths and maintain control of yourself.

Counting to ten also has a corollary: *Take the conflict to a private setting.* Nothing skews an interaction faster or more dangerously than an audience. If your child challenges you in front of a neighbor, if shoppers in the supermarket turn and stare, if your child's friends are in the car, factors such as "losing face," "maintaining one's authority," and "peer pressure" are introduced into what is already a difficult dynamic. In these cases astute bystanders will excuse themselves. If this does not happen, postpone discussion until later or, if that is not possible, excuse yourselves and locate a private spot in which to talk.

Parents often find themselves in what I call the "preconflict" stage. This is when their child has made a remark, taken an action, or posed a question that *threatens* to develop into a conflict. It may also be that the parent has simply observed something—a messy room, a broken bicycle, a valuable belonging left outside. The child may be nowhere to be seen. At these times also, count to ten. You may end up deciding: *It doesn't matter; it isn't my business; if it gets ruined he'll just have to buy a new one,* and a conflict will have been averted.

Let's say, however, that you are in the thick of it. Your fourteen-year-old daughter has just asked if she can go to a rock concert Saturday night with some friends. One of them, a sixteen-year-old who just got his license, will be driving.

"I don't think it's a good idea," you reply.

Your daughter responds angrily. "Are you saying I can't go?"

"I'm just saying—"

"I shouldn't even have to ask you. Just 'cause you stopped drinking you think you can tell me what to do. I liked it better when you were always drunk. I could do what I wanted then."

You can feel the explosive potential of this exchange. COUNT TO TEN! Counting to ten needn't be a secret tactic.

If your daughter pushes you for a response, explain what you are doing by saying:

"I'm taking a few minutes to think so I won't say or do anything I'll regret."

or

"I'm feeling angry and I want to calm down before answering."

You may wish to table the discussion to a less tempestuous time. If this is the case, try to include your daughter in the decision to do so. You don't want her to feel unilaterally dismissed, which might happen if all you said was:

"I'm not going to deal with this now."

or

"I'll give you an answer when I'm ready."

Acknowledge her stake in the issue by explaining:

"I know this is very important to you and that you'd like me to give you an answer now. But I need to think about it a bit. Why don't we calm down and discuss it after dinner."

I mentioned before that not all conflict can be happily resolved. At this point, your daughter may continue a one-sided escalation. She may stomp, swear, and storm out of the house. But she cannot make you answer. You have done the best any parent could do. You can allow your daughter her response and still approach her later to deal with the initial issue, as well as any subsequent issues that evolve from it.

Step 2: Ask Questions

You counted to ten and are now in control of your physical and emotional self. It is time to move to the information-gathering phase of CARE-ful conflict resolution. You do this by asking questions—first, of yourself:

- What am I feeling?
- Do these feelings seem appropriate and proportional to the issues involved?
- What needs am I seeking to express or fulfill through this conflict (e.g., respect, approval, love, control)?
- Am I bringing stereotypes or past baggage to the conflict (e.g., "my son the spoiled brat," "my daughter who doesn't love me," "my own father who used to hit me")?
- Am I displacing emotions from another time or situation onto this one?
- What—specifically—is this conflict about (e.g., values, morals, logistics, opinions, safety, health, power, control, pride)?
- Are the threats to health or safety I perceive real or imagined?

- Are my character defects exacerbating the conflict?
- Am I trying to change my child?
- Are the expectations and limits I'm setting appropriate to my child's age?
- What assumptions have I made about myself, my child, and/or the issues involved? Do I know that these assumptions are valid?
- Am I open to changing my mind? To compromising? To considering other options?
- Am I really listening to my child?

You also need to ask yourself questions *in terms of your child.* You want to try to understand the conflict from her point of view. For example:

- How would my child define the conflict?
- What does my child feel?
- What needs or desires of my child's are being expressed or thwarted?
- What hidden agenda is my child bringing to the issue?
- What baggage from the past is my child carrying?
- How is my child viewing me?

Note that your interpretation of the conflict may not be the same as your child's. In the example cited earlier, you may be most concerned with your daughter's safety. She may be most concerned with her freedom and image in the eyes of her peers. Since she has no problems with a sixteen-year-old driving, she may be surprised to learn that your opposition stems from this factor. She may assume that you don't want her out late, or you don't like her friends, or you're just being mean and trying to control her life.

Therefore, it is essential during this step to ask questions of your child so that you can understand her thoughts and feelings and gather any information that might influence your consideration (What time is the concert? Who else will be going? When will you be home?).

Your child should be encouraged to ask questions too, both of herself and of you. This step lays bare all the issues, so that you and your child, while still not agreeing, are at least looking at the same pieces of the puzzle. The conflict is now out in the open and can be identified.

Step 3: Reflect

You are now surrounded by the raw data of your questioning and introspection: feelings, memories, assumptions, theories, cautions, convictions, and, possibly, new questions. At this point, the conflict can be resolved by any of the following:

- *The situation changes and the issue becomes moot.* The concert is canceled, or your daughter's friends call and say that they can't go. Since this is beyond your control, you cannot plan for it. (Just be grateful when it happens!)

- *One person gives in.* You tell your daughter, "Do whatever you want," in order to avoid a fight. Or your daughter says, "Just forget it! I should've known better than to ask you for permission to do anything." While such responses eliminate the conflict, they don't resolve it. Resentments will only crop up later. Therefore, this approach should be avoided.

- *One person changes his position.* As you reflect, you may discover that an echo from the past is in play. You may uncover fears or expectations that you wish to reject. You may decide that, despite misgivings, the issue isn't that big a deal. You eliminate the conflict by changing your own attitude, behavior, or position. You do so without resentment or martyrdom.

At this point, the conflict may essentially be resolved, although you might have to follow up with a communication to your child and/or further monitoring of your attitudes and actions. If, however, upon reflection, the conflict still remains, you need to negotiate and engage a solution. This occurs in the next step.

Step 4: Engage

This is the final, action step of CARE-ing conflict resolution. It is the coming together, the meshing of everyone's needs and feelings into a solution that works for all. If the conflict is resolvable by making changes within yourself, it is here that you commit to those changes and work to achieve them. If the conflict requires negotiation with others, it is here that you work to solve the problem and follow through with the necessary actions. You may choose to use the problem-solving structure outlined in chapter 18.

In the example here, you and your daughter would brainstorm for solutions that address the issues you uncovered by Asking Questions and Reflecting. Let's say you're concerned about her safety. Your daughter, now that she realizes the source of your opposition, may feel there's hope and be motivated to propose compromises that would lessen, in your eyes, the risk of her going.

Keep in mind that resolving a conflict in this step doesn't mean that there may not be other conflicts lying below the surface of the original one. In the example here, this is clearly the case. A much larger conflict over issues of control and independence exists between father and daughter and must be addressed, along with the hurt and anger fueling it.

CARE is a fluid process. As you become more experienced and comfortable with conflict resolution, you will shift back and forth between the steps, between self- and other-directed questions, between your own internal reality-checks and your child's words and behaviors, between knowledge and supposition. Depending on any number of factors—the nature of the conflict, the age and relationship of the individuals involved, the amount of past baggage called forth—this process may take place instantly, almost unconsciously, with awareness and resolution easily achieved, or it may take place in painful, uncertain fits and starts over days, weeks, or months.

It is always possible that negotiation will fail to produce an acceptable solution. In such cases, you may be able to *Agree to disagree.* This option pertains more to conflicts over taste, opinions, attitudes, and priorities than to practical disputes. For example, if you and your child both need the car at the same time, you can't agree to disagree. One of you is going to get the car and one is not. If, however, one of you believes that baseball is boring and the other does not, you can agree to respect each other's right to an opinion (no matter how dumb you think it is). You can choose to not let the conflict harm your relationship.

When you embrace this four-step approach to resolving conflict, you present your children with a wonderful and useful model. There are several other things you can do to help your children deal with conflict in their own lives.

Encourage Your Children to Use the Four Steps of CARE to Settle Differences among Themselves and with Their Friends

For younger children who are fighting physically, separate them and say:

"We don't hit each other. That's not how we solve our problems. We solve our problems by first taking deep breaths and counting to ten." Then count aloud with them.

When older children scream at each other or come running to you with "Mom, he took my notebook and he won't give it back," say:

"I know that the two of you can solve this problem if you calm down and discuss it. I'd like you to count to ten and then we'll take a look at it." Let them count silently. Then, guide them through the remaining three steps of CARE.

Kids, too, have hidden agendas and displaced emotions. Be on the lookout for them. Don't be surprised if the surface conflict leads through a trail of fourteen other conflicts to a very different issue.

Encourage Your Children to Use the Four Stages of CARE to Deal with Internal Conflict

Many of the dilemmas children face can be addressed with CARE: *Should I go to the dance with Sheila who asked me first and whom I already said yes to or Kathy who asked me today but whom I like better? Should I tell the teacher I saw a gun in Sean's locker? What should I do if there are drugs at the party tomorrow night?*

If your child comes to you for advice, or you see that she is struggling with a problem, the steps of CARE will help her to consider her feelings and options, and make her own decision.

Play the Dilemma Game

This game gives children practice in identifying the various issues, values, and options people face in dealing with internal and/or external conflicts. The game can be played by one child or many. Parents can join in too. Begin by having one of the participants present a moral or practical dilemma to the others. (You might have everyone write down several before the game and put them in a hat.) For example

> Billy has already agreed to sell his jacket to Tom, a classmate at school, for thirty dollars. On his way to give the jacket to Tom and get the thirty dollars, Billy is stopped in the hall by another boy. "Hey," the boy says, "great jacket! I'll give you fifty bucks for it." To whom should Billy sell his jacket and why?

> A friend asks if you'll let him copy off your paper during the math test. You know that this friend is terrible in math and

> *if he brings home a bad grade he'll get beaten by his father.*
> *What would you do?*

Each player's job is to (1) identify the central issues of the conflict and (2) propose a solution. Players are allowed to ask questions of the "dilemma presenter" in order to flesh out their understanding of the people and factors involved. (Does Billy need the money? Are Tom and Billy friends? Who's bigger, Tom or Billy?) Obviously, different players may reach different conclusions, which, in and of itself, is a valuable part of the game.

Find the Conflict

Most books, movies, and television shows revolve around a central conflict: For example, Romeo and Juliet's love is in conflict with the long-standing feud between their families; ET's friendship with Elliot is in conflict with his desire to go back home; Rambo is in conflict with . . . everybody. After your kids read a book or watch a movie or TV show, ask them to identify the conflict(s) that propel the story. Ask them how the central conflict appears to different characters. Ask them how the conflict is resolved and whether they would have resolved it differently. They will probably notice the role violence plays in settling differences, particularly in movies and television. See if they can propose alternate solutions.

Look for newspaper or magazine articles that report conflicts (wars, political debates, social issues, religious differences, lawsuits, and so on). Discuss with your kids what they think the conflict is about and ways in which it might be solved. You might do this by asking:

"If you were President, what would you do?"

or

"If you were the judge, what would your verdict be and why?"

Most kids love to be asked for their opinions and presented

with "brain teasers"—as long as their answers are not judged, criticized, or ridiculed.

This chapter presents a structure for dealing directly with conflict. As you practice the principles discussed in this book, you will discover that the number of conflicts you have to deal with will diminish. As you *Keep it simple,* many issues will no longer lay claim to your priority list. As you remember *This too shall pass,* many problems will, with time, disappear without anyone being the worse off. As you *Live and let live* and *Stop playing God,* you will discover that many conflicts can be eliminated if you let go of your need to control and change other people. As you live *One day at a time,* conflicts provoked by fear and projection will fall away.

It is important to keep in mind that your attempts to resolve family conflict with mutual respect and good faith may not find reciprocation for some time. Your job, however, is not to change your children. Your job is to focus on yourself. Eventually, your children will change. But you will not have made them change. Your honesty, open-mindedness, and love will have made them change themselves.

12

Attraction Rather Than Promotion
Using the Power of Example

While we came into recovery for many reasons, we stayed for one reason: We saw *models* of recovery that we found attractive. We wanted what these people had. We were told to take a seat, to keep coming back. We did. We listened and watched. We saw how these people handled their feelings and problems. We heard them talk about their program and their relationship with a Higher Power. We felt their serenity and joy, their strength and humor. We witnessed honesty and self-awareness, humility and tolerance—not in empty words, but in deed.

So we tried on their thinking and tried out their behavior. We learned by observing—and then by practicing what we observed. When our efforts were rewarded, the learning was reinforced.

Children, also, learn by observing role models. They see their parents drink out of a cup, put on a hat, dial a telephone, play "patty cake," and they imitate the behavior themselves. When kids play soldier, doctor, or house, they are acting out roles they have observed.

Much of this type of learning takes place without the child or parent being aware that it is happening. Indeed, when parents wonder where on earth their child learned some new skill or expression, chances are she learned it from watching them or someone else—a sibling, a peer, a teacher, a stranger on the bus, a character on TV. In fact, much of a child's learning takes place *without the child having a full understanding of its meaning or possible consequences.* The ubiquity of role models, coupled with the subliminal nature of their influence, make modeling one of the most powerful and unpredictable forces of socialization.

The more a child identifies with role models, the more likely she is to adopt their values, attitudes, and behavior. Thus, modeling is simply an avenue for learning. The lessons that travel that avenue can be for good or for bad.

A child's parents are her first and most influential role models. When we were using, we modeled many behaviors for our children: how to avoid problems with a drink or a drug, how to deny reality and repress feelings. When we failed to meet our obligations, we taught irresponsibility; when we lied, we taught dishonesty. Our kids had front-row seats for our versions of love, marriage, communication, and emotional honesty. By watching us, our children acquired many of these attitudes and behaviors themselves.

None of us would deny that our behavior when we were using hurt our kids. But we may tend to think of that behavior in terms of what we *did* rather than what we *taught.* If we are to become better parents in recovery, it is important to think of our actions not only in terms of their direct consequences but in terms of their underlying lessons. For example, if, when we were using, we slapped our child, our behavior hurt him physically and emotionally. Yet the repercussions of this action went beyond these direct consequences, for we presented a model for our child that said: This is how you handle these situations. We demonstrated how to be violent, how to be a bully, how to be out of control. No wonder research shows that children who watch violence, whether in the home or on TV, are more likely to exhibit aggressive behavior themselves and to condone its use as a legitimate way to solve problems than are children not so exposed.

Now, in recovery, we can use the power of modeling to our child's advantage. We can model honesty, compassion, patience, and open-mindedness. We can show how to solve rather than avoid problems.

The power of modeling is a gift to parents. It means we do not have to be great teachers or psychologists to influence our children; we don't have to be masters of persuasion or brilliant analysts of human behavior to improve family relationships; we don't have to "make" our kids be honest, or hardworking, or loving. All we have to do is be these things ourselves.

Our ability to attract our children toward behaviors and attitudes we value will be enhanced by keeping in mind the following guidelines.

Be Warm and Nurturing

Research has shown that children are more likely to be influenced by role models who are warm and nurturing. In addition, they are more likely to adopt the behaviors of those they see as similar to themselves (of similar age, background, interests, values, and so on) and those they see as having power (people with desirable attributes, goodies to dispense, the ability to make things happen). From these characteristics it is clear why parents are such influential role models, particularly in a child's early years.

These characteristics also help to explain the influence peers, siblings, teachers, celebrities, and even cartoon characters can have on a child's socialization—especially if these figures are felt by the child to be warm and nurturing. Note that the child doesn't need to have a "real world" relationship with the model; the relationship can occur solely within the child's mind and heart.

Children who belong to gangs often speak of the gang as their "family," as the place where they are valued and understood. It is not surprising, then, that gangs can play such a large part in shaping the behavior and values of youngsters who do not have strong adult role models in the home.

Studies have shown that children with nurturing models tend to imitate helping behaviors, while children with distant or rejecting models tend to imitate aggressive actions.[7,8,9] This makes sense, for a nurturing parent not only provides her child with the love, security, and attention from which kind and giving acts spring, but also presents a model for caring, prosocial behavior.

Walk the Walk, Don't Talk the Talk

When we were using, we rarely practiced what we preached. We lectured our children on honesty and lied about our own behavior. We failed to meet our responsibilities and yelled at our kids for being irresponsible. We told them smoking was bad and then rushed to the store for a carton of cigarettes.

When they called us on our duplicity we said:

"Do what I say, not what I do."

"It's different; I'm older than you."

And while there is certainly a kernel of truth in the notion that different behaviors are appropriate for different ages, there certainly wasn't the bushel of truth with which we endowed it.

Kids are shrewd judges of character. They know deceit when they smell it. In one experiment, children were exposed to role models who either preached generosity or acted it out.[10] Preaching had no effect on kids' behavior, although it did affect their verbal statements. (In other words, they modeled the hypocrisy!) The children exposed to charitable *behavior,* however, tended to behave charitably themselves. Thus, the child faced with a choice between doing what a parent says and doing what a parent does will generally imitate the behavior.

Show, Don't Tell

We would never think of teaching our child to tie his shoe by simply telling him how to do it. We would show him. (Or buy Velcro sneakers!) We might accompany the lesson with a narration: "You take the two laces and cross them. . . ." But the real learning for the child takes place through watching and practicing.

One of the ways you can attract your child to the traits and attitudes you value is by providing opportunities for him to exercise them. Much of a child's growth occurs by "trying on" new roles and behaviors. For example, good judgment results from exercising one's judgment and seeing what happens. From a parent's perspective, this means letting your child make as many decisions for himself as possible. Often, however, we're tempted to step in and do our child's thinking for him, especially when we see that he is about to make a poor choice. When we do so, we deprive our child of a valuable opportunity to learn. He never experiences the results of his decision—only ours. This can be seen in the following example offered by the recovering mother of a ten-year-old:

"When my daughter was eight, I decided she was old enough to have an allowance. It was a disaster. As soon as she got the money, everywhere we went she wanted to buy the first thing she saw. I was constantly having to tell her no, she couldn't buy this and no, she couldn't buy that. I tried to explain that if she wanted something later in the week, she wouldn't have any money left. I was talking about it with my husband and he said, 'Why don't you just let her buy whatever she wants? If she runs out of money, she runs out of money. And maybe next week she'll think twice before she spends it.'

"It was such a simple solution, I mistrusted it immediately. But I went ahead and let her waste her money. We had a few scenes because I refused to advance her any more. But within a few weeks she seemed much more cautious about spending—and now, you've never seen such a little miser."

Letting our children make their own decisions doesn't mean standing by as they head for disaster. In those circumstances where children could do lasting harm to themselves or others, of course we need to step in. But often, if we walk through the decision with them, if we ask questions that help them identify the likely consequences, they will come to a wise choice. Children want to make good decisions. They don't want to hurt other people.

They don't want to be embarrassed, humiliated, or frightened. These powerful motivations, combined with opportunities to practice decision making, will foster good judgment.

You can use this model to nurture the development of any trait in your child. First, identify the desired trait: responsibility, compassion, generosity, and so on. Then, think of ways in which the trait is exercised, forums in which it is demanded. Finally, create opportunities for your child to practice the trait.

Encourage Your Children to Learn from Other Children

Studies have shown that children learn behaviors they observe in their peers. One study found that socially isolated children became more sociable after watching a film of peers modeling social behavior.[11] Researchers in another study had a group of disruptive children watch and copy the behavior of "good" classmates.[12] The disruptive children were told that this would help them to get along better in school. And it did! A dramatic and durable improvement in behavior was observed.

Studies such as these highlight the modeling power of a child's peers. As parents, we tend to think of this power in negative terms. Just say the words *peer pressure* and most of us get a visceral image of our perfect, darling child being led astray by those delinquents down the street. (Of course, it's never *our* children who are doing the leading!) Naturally, peer pressure can be exerted in antisocial directions. We can, however, use the power of peer modeling as a positive tool in our children's lives, particularly when they are feeling awkward or hesitant about their social skills.

"My child was very ambivalent about trying out for Little League," explained a recovering father of six. "I told him it was up to him. He decided not to, although his best friend from school did join the team. My son ended up watching nearly every practice and game. The next year he couldn't wait to sign up. Out of curiosity, I asked him what had changed his mind. He said, 'Now I know what it's like.'"

A related experience was described by a mother with three years' sobriety. "My daughter was very shy. It wasn't that she was unpopular, she just didn't seem to have any social skills or confidence. One day she confided to me how stupid she felt. She said she never knew what to say, especially now that boys were being drawn into her clique. I suggested that she watch her friends. What did they say and do? I told her to take notes in her mind."

This mother's suggestion was excellent. It recognized the difference between *being with* and *attending to*. Although the girl was present in the social situation, her self-consciousness prevented her from noticing the transactions that were taking place. When she started to pay attention to what was going on, however, she was able to identify behaviors that she could copy.

The next time I saw the mother, she told me what had happened: "Several weeks after making the suggestion, I asked my daughter if she had tried it. She got this big grin on her face and said, 'I found out what they do. The girls just ask the boys about sports or some dumb game that was on TV the night before or how they did on a test, or they tell them they love their shirt or muscles or something, and then the boys just start talking and don't shut up.' So my daughter felt she'd learned the secrets of socializing. I felt like marching over to the school and giving a lecture on sex role stereotypes!"

If your children express feelings of discomfort or inadequacy about certain skills or social interactions, encourage them to watch what their friends do and listen to what their friends say. Of course, this doesn't mean they should blindly model their behavior after someone else's. Help your children to process the information they gather. Ask them what they think about the behavior they observe. Does it work? Does it hurt anybody? Does it make people feel good? Does it feel right for them?

Encourage Older Siblings to Be Models
for Younger Brothers and Sisters

We set siblings up to be rivals when we say:

"You're older than she is. You should know better."

"I don't care if he started it. I expect more from you."

"Why can't you be more like your brother? Do you see him acting like such a baby?"

Comments such as these turn the age difference into a weapon we use *against* our kids rather than a tool we use *for* our kids. Young children have a natural tendency to idolize older children and to adopt their behavior. Help your older kids to see the advantages in this law of nature. They can influence their pesky younger siblings, not by tormenting them but by modeling the behaviors they'd like to see.

One teenager of a recovering parent was furious because her six-year-old brother kept barging into her room without knocking. When she wasn't there, he often took things of hers without asking.

"Do you knock when you go into his room?" I asked.

"No," she said. "He doesn't care."

"Do you take his things without asking?"

"He doesn't have anything I want."

I suggested that she try an experiment. "Make a point of knocking on your brother's door, even if it's open. Wait for him to say you can come in. If he says you don't have to knock, tell him that you want to knock because it's polite and respectful of his privacy. Then ask his permission to borrow something."

"What if I don't want anything?"

"Make something up. The point is for him to observe how you act in these situations. That may be all you'll need for him to start knocking on your door. If not, remind him that you'd appreciate it if he knocked just like you do."

A few weeks later I asked her if things were any better.

"A little," she said. "He almost always knocks on my door now, but he still sometimes takes things when I'm not there. When I told him I wanted him to ask me first he said, 'But then you might say no.' I guess he figures he's not doing anything wrong if he doesn't give me the chance to say no."

"Keep at it," I said. "Progress not perfection, you know."

"Now, where have I heard that before?" she said.

13

Rigorous Honesty
Encouraging Healthy Communication with Our Children

When we were drinking and drugging, our lives were polluted with dishonesty. We lied about where we had been and where we were going. We lied about what we said, thought, and did. We lied to evade responsibility and avoid the consequences of our mistakes. We even lied about our lies: *They're not really lies since I wouldn't have to tell them if people didn't bug me all the time.*

Dishonesty infected our relationships with our children and destroyed the trust that is essential to healthy parent-child relationships. If we are to restore our children's trust in us, we must place honesty at the center of our relationship with them.

Being honest is difficult for addicts. Those of us who grew up in troubled homes learned to be dishonest at a young age. Our parents, with their lies and deceptions, taught us how to deny reality and disavow feelings. Dishonesty became a way of life, a defense against humiliation and punishment.

Even now, in recovery, we still have trouble being honest. "Sometimes I find myself lying without even knowing I'm doing it," said a recovering mother of two. "The other day my kids were helping me to unpack the groceries and when they got to the last bag, they asked me where the ice cream was. Without missing a beat, I said, 'They were out of it.' The reality was I had forgotten it.

My kids gave me this look like, *Who ever heard of a supermarket running out of ice cream?* I know they didn't believe me. I don't know why I do this. It's a real problem for me."

Said another recovering parent: "I'm forever inventing traffic jams and dead batteries to explain why I'm late. I know I should just say, 'I'm sorry I'm late; I didn't allow enough time to get here,' but I can't."

Becoming honest takes time and patience. We must listen to our words as we speak them and, if need be, stop in the middle of a sentence, go back, and correct our misrepresentation. The sighs I hear when parents speak about trying to break the habit of dishonesty reflect the degree to which they recognize it as the addict's inertial state.

Force of habit is not, however, the only reason for the perpetuation of dishonesty in our lives. We are also afraid to be honest. We are afraid to recognize the envy, hurt, or hatred we sometimes feel. We don't want to acknowledge errors from our past. Many of us took our first moral inventory and thought we came out pretty much unscathed. Then, as we became more honest, we took a second inventory and were astonished to see how many wrongs we had missed, feelings we had forgotten.

Before we decide that "honesty is the best policy" with our children, we have to admit that deep down, we don't believe in that policy ourselves. Honesty got us into trouble as kids. We associate being honest with admitting mistakes, confessing sins, getting punished. We are afraid that rigorous (read: brutal) honesty will injure feelings and ruin friendships. And this is certainly possible if we think of honesty as a license to kill.

Some parents, while dishonest in many areas of their lives, have no trouble being "honest" with their children. This form of honesty is defined as *Telling my kids everything that is wrong with them.* These same parents are generally not honest about revealing themselves. They hide their faults, feelings, and concerns with the rationalization "I don't want my child to worry. She's too young to understand." Sometimes this caution is justified. But more often than not, children are already worried, and their concern would be better served by honest words appropriate to their level of understanding than by deception.

Parents also fear that being honest about themselves will result in a loss of face or authority; they don't want any intimations of human frailty to undercut their role as disciplinarian. Thus, the children of such parents have their emotional candle burned at both ends; not only do they hear a litany of their imperfections but they hear it from "perfect" parents.

In order to become more honest in our relationships, we need to stop thinking of honesty as cold, hard truth. We also need to abandon the notion that being honest with children means taking their inventories. Instead, we need to think of honesty as sharing our feelings, ideas, and mistakes and allowing our children to share theirs—without fear of rejection or recrimination. Honesty means expressing affection and making amends, recognizing strengths and achievements. It is moral fresh air—healthy, cleansing, and restorative.

Rigorous honesty is the basis for all healthy communication and relationships. Such honesty involves being on the lookout for hidden agendas.

Hidden Agendas

Hidden agendas are the feelings, needs, and motives that remain unknown or unstated during conflicts and conversations. If we use lavish gifts to buy love or pay off guilt, our action is motivated by a hidden agenda. If we deny our child freedoms appropriate to his age—if we keep him a "baby" so that we don't have to confront our anxieties over aging—this action, too, comes from a hidden agenda.

Hidden agendas can also emanate from loving, supportive motives. For example, a mother may invite neighborhood children over in an attempt to help her shy daughter become more comfortable with her peers—without telling her why she is doing so. A father may lie to his son about his health to spare the boy worry. Whether hidden agendas stem from "positive" or "negative" motivations, the potential for harm still remains, especially if none of the people involved is aware that such agendas exist.

"When I was in early recovery," said a forty-one-year-old mother, "I had huge arguments with my daughter about dating. I was sharing this with my sponsor and she said, 'Your daughter's the most responsible sixteen-year-old I know. So what's going on?' It got me thinking, and I realized that I was jealous. It was that simple. I was divorced; I hadn't been out with anybody for three years; and here was my beautiful, bright daughter with every boy in school at her feet. It was like a mirror held up to my own life and it hurt. I felt so small for feeling that way. You want your kids to be happy and popular—and then you realize that on another level you don't."

This is not the sort of hidden agenda you would necessarily share with your child. But you need to share it with yourself.

Children can also bring hidden agendas to their interactions with parents. The "problem child" may be acting the role as a means of getting attention; the adolescent who insists he needs a room of his own "in order to study" may be motivated by a desire for increased privacy; the child who's "sick" every Monday and Wednesday may be avoiding the showers in gym.

Hidden agendas are tricky to deal with. We all—parents and children alike—are entitled to our private thoughts, feelings, and motivations. Not every hidden agenda need or should be exposed. But we must make every effort to be aware of the inner forces that affect our actions and attitudes, and to help our children do the same for themselves. Otherwise, we risk building our relationships on a bedrock of dishonesty.

There are several things parents can do to keep hidden agendas from blocking intimacy and effective problem solving:

Discuss the Idea of Hidden Agendas with Your Kids

Explain to your kids that people's feelings, actions, and words are often influenced by forces they're not aware of or that they keep hidden from others. Offer some examples of situations in which your own behavior was influenced by hidden agendas. See if your children can come up with their own:

"I was nice to Marcie because I wanted to get invited to her party."

"I ran for student council because it meant I could get out of study hall."

"I didn't take out the rubbish because I was mad at you for not buying me a new guitar."

Be on the Alert for Hidden Agendas

When little sparks trigger big conflicts, when feelings and reactions seem disproportionate to the issue at stake, chances are good that hidden agendas are afoot. Seek them out. First, look within yourself. Next, consider whether your child may be bringing hidden agendas to the table. It is important to do this without accusing her of being deceptive or blind to her feelings and motivations. The best approach is a nonpersonalized one:

"What do you think the real issue is here?"

"Are there any other things you're thinking or feeling that you'd like to bring up?"

If you've discussed the idea of hidden agendas, you can be even more direct:

"Do you think there's a hidden agenda here?"

Pay Attention to Your Child's Life

The more aware you are of your child's life, the more likely you are to sense whether a hidden agenda is influencing her words or behavior. By showing interest in your child, and by listening supportively to the concerns and events she shares, you will have a better idea of her inner and outer worlds. This knowledge will help you to understand any social, emotional, or practical forces affecting your relationship.

Ask questions, but don't grill. Express interest, but don't pry. Rote questions such as "How was school?" or "What did you do today?" tend to generate rote answers such as "Okay" and "Nuthin'." Vary your questions to keep them fresh and to encourage thoughtful answers:

"What did you daydream about in school today?"

"Did anything unfair/surprising/dangerous happen to you today?"

Seek out your child's opinions about, and reactions to, people and events. Accept her comments without judgment. Let your child know you enjoy hearing her news:

"I'm really glad you told me that."

"I love hearing about your day/friends/classes."

One way of telling whether you're in touch with your child's life is by giving yourself a little quiz. For instance:

- What is your child's favorite subject in school?
- What subject is your child having the most trouble with?
- Who are your child's heroes?
- Who is your child's best friend?
- What does your child collect?
- What does your child want to be when she grows up?
- What does your child do when she goes out with her friends?
- What is your child's favorite book/movie/record?
- What does your child worry about?
- What would your child like to change about herself?
- What would your child like to change about you?

If you can't answer questions such as these, you need to get more involved in your child's world.

How to Communicate Honestly with Your Children

Many recovering parents feel that they will never be able to open a path of communication with their children. This feeling is a natural response to the problems and pain that have characterized their families. Fortunately, communication can be restored if parents are willing to change the ways in which they speak and listen.

Encourage Your Children to Talk

When parents don't listen, kids stop talking. Listening is hard work. It requires energy and focus. If our children come to talk to us and we continue to read the paper, watch the news, or work at our desk, we are not listening. We are not listening if, when our children speak, we carry on an internal conversation with ourselves: daydreaming, challenging, fuming, rebutting.

Minds wander. It is what they do best. Thus, the first step in good communication is giving your full attention to your children when they speak. This takes willingness—willingness to hear their words, understand their feelings, and see things from their point of view.

The essence of encouraging children to talk comes down to this: *Children talk when they feel safe doing so.* You can create this climate of safety in a number of ways.

- *Be patient.* It takes kids time to compose their thoughts. Don't finish your child's sentences for her. If you seem impatient, your child may assume she's boring you.
- *Be available.* Your kids are going to come to you at all sorts of inconvenient times. But if their need is real, be thrilled that they do come and try to seize the moment. If you are truly unavailable, say so, but be sure to let your child know that you really do want to hear what he has to say. Commit to precise times when you can get together, and be sure to follow through.

   In the same way that we used to try to distract our teachers from the day's lesson with irrelevant questions, your child may try to manipulate you by bringing up "important things" at self-serving times such as bedtime or homework time. If this happens, you can say: "I'd like to talk about that, but this isn't the time. We can talk tomorrow morning (or after your chores are done, and so on)."

- *Keep your mouth shut.* Just because your child says something doesn't mean he wants a lecture in return. Don't feel you have to offer the quick fix or teach one of life's lessons every time your child comes to you with a problem or a plan. Just listen, reflect, empathize, and accept.

- *Don't tattle.* If your child tells you something in confidence, keep it confidential. Naturally, you may need to violate this confidentiality if what your child tells you indicates that he or someone else is in serious trouble or danger (e.g., a suicidal sibling, an abused friend). But in cases such as these, you should first try to help your child see why the circle of confidence needs to be enlarged.

  By the same token, don't push and probe into areas in which your child feels uncomfortable; it will only drive him away. Instead of prying, you can say: "I'd like to talk to you about that, but I understand if you'd rather not. If you change your mind, I'd be happy to discuss it."

- *Hear your remarks before you say them.* Listening to what you are about to say from your child's point of view will tell you whether you're being destructive or constructive. For example, if your child says: "I got cut from the swim team today," and you answer, "Well, cheer up. There's always next year," you're denying the hurt and disappointment he feels now. If you say, "What a shame! I'm so upset to hear that," you're giving the poor kid the additional burden of having made you feel lousy.

Stick to simple reflective listening: "You got cut from the team?" (This invites further talking, further explanations.) "It really meant a lot to you to be on the team." (Empathy invites your child to unload his feelings.) "I can see that it's really got you down." (It's okay to be bummed out. You love your child whether his news is good or bad.)

- *Tune in to body language.* When words are untruthful, body language gives us away. Pay attention to your own body language when you speak. If your chin is tight, your hands are clutched, your eyes are hot, your child will feel your anger regardless of the content of your words.

  Tune in to your child's body language too. If you're speaking and your child is drumming his fingers, rolling his eyeballs, playing with a pencil, don't pounce on him like a mind reader, but do act like a parent concerned about the quality of communication taking place. For example, you might say: "Do you feel uncomfortable talking about this?" or "Are you angry about what I'm saying?" This gives your child permission to feel and express his anger. If your child is fidgety and distracted, you might say: "I'd like to discuss this at a time when you are able to pay attention. Can you do that now?" ("If not, when?")

Use the Skills of Active Listening

1. Show that you're tuned in by nodding and making eye contact.
Nonverbal gestures such as a hug, a squeeze of the hand, or a pat on the back can all convey empathy. Obviously, these may not be possible or appropriate if your child is extremely agitated or hostile.

2. **Express support with an occasional grunt, hmmm, yup, or uh-huh.**

Expressions such as "Go on," "What happened then?" or "No kidding!" can help your child to feel that you are attending to what she is saying. Again, you need to be sensitive to the appropriateness and naturalness of your comments in light of the affect and content of your child's statements.

These two techniques show your child that you are listening. The following two show that you understand and accept what she says.

3. **Reflect the feelings behind your child's words.**

If your child says: "I hate you. It's not fair. You can't tell me what to do!" don't respond to the words. Respond to the feeling:

"You're angry that I won't let you go to the party."

Such a response facilitates the honest expression of emotion. If you were to reply: "You'll do what you're told" or "How dare you speak to me like that!" you might show your child who's boss, but you'd do little to further communication.

In addition to reflecting your child's feelings, you can reflect the factual content of her words:

"You tried to explain but the teacher wouldn't listen?"

"You left it on the table and when you came back it was gone?"

This type of reflective listening keeps your child talking, verifies the accuracy of your understanding, and allows your child to correct any misimpressions you may have received.

4. **Keep an ear open for your child's "stinkin' thinkin'."**

Help your child to identify the shoulds, musts, and awfuls that propel her emotional upsetments (see chapter 9). It's important that you do this in a supportive rather than critical manner. Watch the difference between the two in the following interactions:

"I'm going to kill myself if I don't get asked to the dance."

"Don't be silly. It won't be the end of the world. There'll be other dances."

"There won't be any other eighth-grade dances!"

"You've already been to several this year. Missing one won't hurt you. Now stop sulking and go set the table."

"I'm not sulking. And how do you know whether it'll hurt me or not? You don't know how I feel. You don't understand. I'm never going to tell you anything again!"

Now, contrast that scenario with this one:

"I'm going to kill myself if I don't get asked to the dance."

"Not going would be so awful you wouldn't want to live?"

"Well, that's how I'd feel."

"It sure would be disappointing not to be asked."

"I'll say. I thought Steven was going to ask me but he's going with Debby. And I think Brian likes me but he's too scared to ask."

"You could ask Brian."

"I couldn't do that. Hmm, you think? Really? Maybe I will. Thanks for the idea."

The first parent attacked her child. She challenged the child's feelings, labeling them as silly, overblown, and immature. The discussion quickly degenerated into an argument. The one-day-at-a-time parent, however, accepted her child's feelings. She reflected them back in a neutral way so that the child could hear them. The child was not placed on the defensive. This enabled her to see that it wouldn't be the most terrible thing in the world if she didn't go to the dance, even though it would be disappointing. This more rational understanding led the way to a potential solution.

When you respond nonjudgmentally, you invite your child's honesty and trust. Remember that children begin life by being emotionally honest. Nothing is more emotionally honest than a howl of distress, a tantrum, or a hug. A young child doesn't know that what he is feeling is called fear, or anger, or love. He just feels. We are the ones who assign the labels and value judgments. We are the ones who determine how our children come to regard, understand, and deal with their emotions. With this thought in mind, consider some of the statements parents make and the powerful messages these statements convey to children:

Parent Statement	Message Child Hears
"Don't be such a crybaby."	I shouldn't cry.
"Don't you dare get angry with me."	I'm not allowed to feel anger.
"If you can't be cheerful, go to your room."	My parents love me only when I'm cheerful.
"If you feel that way, you're crazy."	Either my feelings are wrong or I'm crazy.

Statements such as these cause kids to (1) clam up, (2) disavow their feelings, and (3) think something's wrong with them. Parents should never label their children's feelings as silly, disproportionate, or wrong. Instead, parents should respond to their children's feelings with statements of empathy ("It must be tough to feel so lonely"; "I know how embarrassing that must have felt") and/or statements that represent the parents' feelings ("I'm sorry that you're still angry with me after so much time has passed").

When you listen for and accept the feelings behind your child's words, you help your child to be emotionally honest. Let's say two siblings are fighting. One of them screams at the other: "You're stupid and ugly and I hate you and I wish you were dead."

Many parents would hook into this child's *words* and say: "Don't you dare talk to your sister that way. I won't have it. You apologize to her immediately and go to your room until dinner." Such a response brings the parent into the middle of the fight—the child is likely to either refuse to apologize or to do so in an insincere manner—and the parent now has the child's "attitude" and "disobedience," as well as the original problem, to contend with.

A one-day-at-a-time parent, however, would recognize her child's outburst as a sign of underlying emotional turmoil. She would say: "You must be very upset to say such hurtful things to your sister, since I know you're not the sort of person who likes to hurt people's feelings. Tell me what the problem is."

Whatever the cause of the argument, the parent, by cueing in to her child's emotions, is now in a position to help him deal with his feelings and make amends to his sister.

Dealing with Dishonesty

One indication that children don't feel safe enough to communicate honestly is when they lie. Of course, all children lie, and your child's telling an occasional fib is not a cause for alarm. If, however, your child lies chronically, it is a symptom of a deeper problem. Many parents become obsessed with unearthing each and every lie, uncovering the truth, and wrenching an admission of guilt from the child. This is an unproductive approach to the problem. In order to help your child stop lying, you need to focus on the underlying issues motivating the lies.

Children lie for a number of reasons:

- *Lying to avoid punishment.* Research shows that this is by far the most common reason for lying. It's interesting that our system of justice is based upon the premise that the accused do not have to testify against themselves. Yet we ask our children to do so all the time. Why *should* a child tell the truth if he's going to be punished for it? Would we admit to a mistake if it meant a beating or a public humiliation—if we could lie our way out of it?

  Lies to avoid punishment stop when we stop punishing our children. We need to respond to our children's wrongdoings with understanding and patience. We need to allow our children to experience the logical consequences of their behavior. In this way, they will discover that taking responsibility for their actions and making amends are not only the right things to do, but the things that will make them feel right with themselves.

- *Lying to inflate their status with peers.* We're all guilty of this: when the fish we hooked somehow gains six inches every time we retell the tale; when the celebrity we spoke with for thirty seconds turns into our "good friend." Children may exaggerate their parents' accomplishments or financial status; they may claim ownership of nonexistent possessions; they may boast of experiences they never had. When such lying becomes chronic, it can lead to

loss of friendships and a blurring of the child's awareness of the truth. This type of lie indicates underlying
problems with self-esteem.

In such cases, parents need to intensify the support
and encouragement they extend to their child. Children
who feel accepted and comfortable with their own identity do not need to tell lies to inflate their status and
self-image.

- *Lying to maintain privacy.* Mark Twain, in "Advice to
Youth," counseled children to "always obey your parents,
when they are present." Children who, when out of their
parents' presence, do something they're not supposed
to, are disinclined to discuss it with their folks. In fact,
lying by omission and word games is a specialty with
adolescents:

> Parent: *Young man, have you been out drinking beer
> with your friends again?*
>
> Child: *No way, Dad. (We weren't out, we were inside;
> and it wasn't beer, it was vodka.)*

You can minimize this form of lying by doing several things:

1. Never respond with ridicule or rejection when your child
reveals something about himself.
2. Avoid intrusive questioning about your child's personal life.
Extend to your child the privacy and autonomy appropriate to his age. The safer your child feels in talking to you, the
smaller the wall of privacy he will need to erect.
3. Don't entrap your child into a lie. If you saw your child at
the mall when he told you he would be studying at the library, don't create an occasion for lying by asking your child
where he was. Simply tell him what you saw and deal with
it from there.
4. Don't be overly restrictive. Many adolescents lie in order to
do things their parents won't let them do. Of course,

teenagers must have limits and where these limits should be is often a matter of debate. Establish a clear relationship between trust and freedom, and your teenagers will put their energy into building trust rather than breaking it.

5. Don't be your child's Lord High Executioner. Teenagers have a strong sense of fairness. If their errors in judgment and behavior are dealt with fairly (e.g., making amends, logical consequences), your children will feel little need to hide their behavior from you—even if they know it will displease you.

- *Lying because that's what Mom and Dad do.* Rare is the child in an alcoholic family who does not grow up with an excellent parental role model for lying. If your child lies, you need to be honest about the example you may have set: The denial of addiction was lying. Calling in sick to work when you were hung over was lying. Telling your family you had to stay late at the office and then going to a bar was lying. Thus, one of the most powerful things you can do to help your child stop lying is to stop lying yourself.

The way you listen determines the way your children talk— whether they confide or close down, explain or evade, lie or tell the truth. But listening to your children is only half the equation. You also want your children to listen to you. And they will—if you talk in such a way that they feel it is safe to do so.

How to Encourage Your Children to Listen

There's one proverb that gets my vote for being the most ridiculous utterance I've ever heard:

Sticks and stones may break my bones
But names will never hurt me.

What a crock! Ask any kid. A broken bone mends a lot faster than a broken spirit. When parents sling verbal stones, children stop listening. They learn that it isn't safe to listen. If we want our children to hear and accept our thoughts and feelings, we need to express them in nonblaming, nonhurtful ways.

We did a lot of attacking when we were using. Our need to control, our perfectionism and impatience, our anger and irritability made us yell, scold, shame, and judge:

"You never show any responsibility."

"You're being a baby."

"You ought to be ashamed of yourself!"

"You show more courtesy to strangers than you do to your own parents."

All these blaming, hurtful statements have one thing in common: the word *you*. *You* did it. *You* let me down. *You're* no good. Phrases like this make kids feel injured and defensive. Parents attack; kids attack back; the discussion loses all touch with the issues as insults fly and outrage escalates.

We've all heard the expression "It's not what you say, it's how you say it." Well, "You-statements" are a lousy way of saying something. They often spring from stinkin' thinkin'. Does our child really *never* do what she's told or show any responsibility around the house? Of course not. But that's what we just told her. No wonder she tunes us out if our statements are so extreme and irrational.

When I suggest to parents that they give up speaking to their children in such ways, they often respond with a look of incredulity:

"You mean I'm not allowed to tell my child that she's done something wrong?"

The fact that we imagine ourselves mute if we can't offer "constructive criticism" proves how dependent we have become on this destructive style of communicating. Ridding our speaking style of "You-statements" doesn't mean that we can't utter a peep to our kids when things bother us. All it means is that instead of telling our children what is wrong with them, we will tell them how we feel about their behavior and its consequences. You can see the difference in the following chart:

Blameful "You-statement"	Respectful "I-statement"
"You never think of anyone except yourself."	"When I make a request and don't get any response, I feel ignored and hurt."
"Who do you think I am, the maid?"	"I would like to get more help with household responsibilities."
"How could you be so careless?"	"I'm angry that you left my book out in the rain."
"Don't you ever take something from my purse without asking!"	"I expect you to ask before taking anything from my purse."

Sometimes, when parents first begin to use "I-statements" to express their feelings, they make the mistake of simply camouflaging a "You-statement." For example, they'll say:

"I feel *you don't ever do what you're told.*"

or

"I feel *you're a selfish, spoiled brat.*"

These are still attacking, blaming "You-statements." These sentiments, restated as true "I-statements" would be:

"I'm upset that you ignored what I said."

"I'm angry that you're not willing to help me."

The focus in each of these statements is on the parent's feelings. "Yes, but you're still talking about the kid," parents sometimes say. Of course. There wouldn't be a statement to make if the child hadn't done (or not done) something. But in an "I-statement," the child's behavior is an event, not a scarlet letter burned into his forehead.

Another thing to note is that each of the above two "I-statements" contains an assumption: the first is that the child "ignored" the parent; the second is that the child is "not willing" to help. These assumptions may be true. But you need to be careful that conflicts do not arise, or become exacerbated, because of erroneous assumptions. Ask questions. Get the facts. It may be that your child truly did not hear you ask her to do something or that she thought it was all right to do it later—both of which are different from ignoring you.

I don't mean to suggest that honest, nonaccusative communication will automatically eliminate conflict and hurt from parent-child interactions. But the more we focus on creating a safe environment for communicating, the more likely we are to get to the core of the problem. If communication fails to resolve a conflict, there are several things you can do:

- *Talk to your kids about "You-statements" and "I-statements."* Make it a family goal to use these respectful, non-hurtful speaking styles. This means being self-conscious about the way you talk to one another for as long as it takes. If you see that you are verbally attacking your child, stop. Rephrase what you were saying. If your child attacks you, ask her to state her complaint in a less hurtful manner, in terms of what she feels about your action rather than in terms of what you are.

  Of course this can be awkward for parent and child alike. But better awkward than destructive. You can even turn the task of improving communication into a car game. One person makes a You-statement: "You never say anything nice to me"; "You always grab the biggest cookie"; "You're a pus-filled, puke-stained wart on the face of humanity!" The other people have to turn each statement into a nonaccusative I-statement. (The game should be prefaced by the disclaimer that any resemblance between the content of the You-statement and family members is purely coincidental!)

- *Agree to disagree.* Accept a standoff. You have expressed your feelings. Your child has expressed hers. The important thing may be that you each know where the other stands and move on from there.

- *Solve the problem.* Bring the conflict to a family meeting. Use the structure suggested in chapter 18 for problem solving. This more formal approach, plus the input of others, may lead to a solution.
- *Table the issue.* Give people a chance to calm down and reflect. Creative problem solving requires time for ideas to incubate, to bubble in the back of one's consciousness. If you sleep on it or come back to the issue in a few days, a fresh outlook may lead to previously unseen solutions.
- *Put your foot down.* When the consequences of an action would be dire and irreversible or would threaten the safety of family members and friends, you may need to exercise a parental veto. In these cases, acknowledge your child's point of view: "I know that you don't agree, and I know that you are very angry with me, but I had to make a decision. I'm sorry we weren't able to find a solution that pleased everyone."

14

Live and Let Live
Learning to Accept Our Children and Ourselves

Our recovery began when we admitted our powerlessness over alcohol and other drugs. Out of this surrender came, not passivity and humiliation, but strength and growth. We discovered that as we accepted ourselves, we became more accepting of others. The unbearable tension we had known in our days of using—in which we railed against people, places, and things over which we had no control—gave way to a new philosophy: *Live and let live.*

When we live and let live, we lighten up and let go of the past. We look life squarely in the eye, and if we don't like what we see, we ask: "Can I do anything about this?" If the answer is yes, we get to work. If the answer is no, we stop beating our head against the wall. Nowhere is this healthy attitude toward life stated more succinctly or eloquently than in the Serenity Prayer:

> *God grant me the SERENITY*
> *To accept the things I cannot change,*
> *The COURAGE to change the things I can,*
> *And the WISDOM to know the difference.*

This prayer should be posted by the bedside of every parent, for many of the burdens of parenthood are unnecessary ones brought on by not knowing what we can and can't "change" about our children.

Acceptance creates the best climate for the growing of healthy children and family relationships. Unfortunately, such a climate is missing in many families, as the following parental remarks show:

"Shame on you."

"It's silly to feel that way."

"I don't care what you think."

"Why do you want to waste your money on that?"

Where there is little or no acceptance, children feel that they are under constant scrutiny:

"Stand up straight."

"Stop fidgeting."

"Get your elbows off the table."

"Can't you do anything right?"

Of course, an occasional criticism, rejection, or non-PC (Properly Communicated) statement isn't going to cause a child any lasting harm. But in many families these types of remarks form the bulk of communication. Since the child does not have the maturity to separate his behavior from his being, his goodness from his gaffes, what he hears in the drip, drip, drip of his parents' criticism is this: *We do not love you. We do not think you're a good person.* The child does not have the insight to think: *Mom and Dad never learned how to express their feelings without going on the attack, and I know that their being on my case all the time doesn't really mean they don't love me; it just means they have this thing about control. . . .*

When a child feels that his worth is measured in terms of what he does, he lives with the constant fear that he will do something wrong and be loved the less for it. Such fear inhibits the risk taking that growth requires. It stands in the way of experimentation, creativity, and passion. It tends to produce one of two responses in the child: submission or rebellion. Neither makes for a healthy child or parent-child relationship.

When we first heard the expression *Live and let live,* it was not followed by an exclusionary clause: Does not apply to children.

Live and let live applies *especially* to children, because children, of all people, are least able to stick up for their rights.

"But what does it mean to 'accept my child'?" parents often ask. "You say, 'Live and let live,' but that doesn't mean I have to accept it if my kid is playing drums at three in the morning, does it?"

Acceptance is not permissiveness. "Accepting" a child does not mean accepting behavior that is rude, cruel, or destructive. Acceptance is love, understanding, encouragement, respect. One way parents express love and respect for their children is by modeling acceptable behavior, by setting limits, and by allowing their kids to experience and redress the consequences of their actions.

While you might expect the child who feels accepted to think: *Great! Now I can do whatever I want,* what happens is just the opposite. Acceptance leads the child to want to become the best version of himself that he can be. He wants to be good, wise, and self-disciplined. He wants to extend to his parents and friends the respect and tolerance they extend to him. This is because acceptance fosters confidence, self-esteem, and courage. Aren't those the foundations of growth upon which we have built our new lives?

There are three forms of acceptance that relate to child rearing:

1. Accepting ourselves as parents.
2. Accepting the nature of things.
3. Accepting our children.

The first two forms of acceptance take place primarily within ourselves. When we accept ourselves as parents, we accept that we have a short fuse, or that we find it difficult to be physically affectionate, or that we made parenting mistakes in the past. This doesn't mean that we can't make amends or become more patient or loving. It simply means that we accept what happened and where we are now.

At the same time that we accept our weaknesses as parents, it is only fair that we recognize our strengths: We tell wonderful bedtime stories; our house is the favorite neighborhood teen hangout; we are good providers.

The acceptance we extend to ourselves as parents puts us in a serene frame of mind. This serenity is reinforced when we practice the second type of acceptance: accepting "the nature of things." By this I mean human nature, parent nature, child nature, the nature of parent-child relationships, and so on.

For example, we accept that babies need to have their diapers changed. Since there is nothing we can do about this design flaw, we attend to our business or, more properly, *their* business, without feeling resentful or angry.

We accept that babies cry, scream, throw food, and get into things they're not supposed to. We accept that toddlers have temper tantrums, that teenagers test us. Again, acceptance doesn't mean passivity, nor does it mean we have to like what we accept. In fact, acceptance often propels us to action—when we child-proof the house, when we sit down and talk out our differences with our fifteen-year-old. Acceptance leads to problem solving and change.

It is when we don't accept the nature of things that relationships break down and, in the extreme, child abuse occurs. Parents who beat their children because the child "wouldn't stop crying" or "wouldn't obey" are enraged because they cannot control their child's behavior. Yet it is in a child's nature to cry and disobey. For parents to expect otherwise is to set themselves up for a war they cannot win.

One-day-at-a-time parents accept that children and adults have different priorities and interests. They recognize that parents and kids, having grown up under different cultural influences, will display different tastes in fashion and music; they will have different historical reference points, different heroes, different ways of looking at things.

Parenthood seems to obliterate memory. The parent who can't stand his child's music forgets that *his* parents couldn't stand the Beatles, and *their* parents couldn't stand Elvis, and *their* parents couldn't stand swing—all the way back to the father of Pan who told the young god, "Dammit, Pan, do you have to play those infernal pipes all day?"

One-day-at-a-time parents realize that much of the conflict between parents and kids is generational. Such conflict, although it becomes personalized, is really propelled by the different life stages and agendas of adults and children. It is natural for parents experiencing a midlife crisis to resent or be jealous of their child's youth, passion, idealism, options, and relative lack of responsibilities. It is natural for children to push the boundaries, to turn to their peers for company and comfort, to view their parents as rigid or overprotective.

It is in the nature of children to be noisy, egocentric, forgetful, irresponsible, inconsiderate, and immature. We must never forget Webster's definition of children:

> *n. a species of little people who slam doors, talk with their mouths full, and track dirt across the kitchen floor.*

Children do not act this way in order to annoy their parents. They act this way because they are children. And it bothers us, not because there is something inherently wrong, immoral, or dangerous in such behavior, but because we experience it as adults (*n. a species of big people who place inordinate emphasis on cleanliness, orderliness, and obedience*).

It is equally in the nature of children to be quiet, generous, empathic, responsible, and considerate—when they are loved, respected, and allowed to grow according to nature's timetable.

When you accept the nature of things, you seek serenity rather than conflict. You let go of battles whose sole purpose is to establish the supremacy of the parent's or child's position—when each position is appropriate to its respective holder. You agree to disagree. You stop trying to change what cannot be changed.

The third form of acceptance is that which we extend to our children. While we also feel this within ourselves, its primary energy is directed outward. Before looking at how we communicate this acceptance, let's examine its internal component.

Within ourselves we need to accept our children as they are. This means accepting that they are shy (or outgoing), clumsy (or coordinated), gifted (or average, or below average). We accept that they are short or tall, poised or awkward, selfish or generous. We accept all their quirks and charms, their strengths and weaknesses, their thoughts and feelings. We must feel this acceptance in our own minds and hearts before we can communicate it to our children.

Creating a Climate of Acceptance

We accept our kids the way they are because we cannot change them. We cannot *make* them more extroverted, studious, or responsible. What we can do is create an environment that supports and values such behavior. We can provide opportunities for them to make decisions and exercise judgment. We can help them to find the courage and desire necessary to change themselves. How? By creating a climate of acceptance. You can do this in many ways.

Don't Stereotype Your Child

Avoid labeling your child's entire being:
  "Don't be such a bully."
  "You're a selfish, spoiled brat."

Such blanket labeling teaches children that if they do something bad, they *are* bad; that if they make a stupid mistake, they *are* stupid. Instead, focus on your child's specific behavior:

  "Leaving your homework on the bus was a forgetful thing to do."
  "You hurt your sister's feelings when you called her those names."

By the same token, be careful about positive stereotyping. The child told, "You're such a good girl," is equally constrained by such labeling because it reinforces the idea that one is either all good or all bad—depending upon one's behavior. The child concludes that if doing something good makes her a "good girl," doing something bad makes her a "bad girl." Similarly, a youngster identified as a "brave boy" will decide that if he feels afraid, he must be a "cowardly boy." This type of stereotyping causes children to link their sense of self-worth to performance. Thus, the child's self-worth is on the line every time he takes an action or tries something new. This conditional self-acceptance—born of the parents' conditional acceptance—discourages children from taking risks or attempting anything at which they might fail.

While the dangers of positive stereotyping are certainly nowhere near as great as those of negative stereotyping, they are part of the same fabric. Parents should be aware that blanket labeling of any kind rarely benefits a child.

Allow Your Child Her Feelings

Don't try to talk your child out of her feelings. This doesn't mean you have to agree with them or even believe they're justified. Acceptance simply means you grant your child the right to feel what she feels. Isn't that what you want for yourself? To see the power of this type of acceptance, consider the following example:

> *Your child comes home at 1:00 A.M., two hours late.*
>
> *"Where have you been?" you scream. "I've been worried sick about you!"*
>
> *"That's stupid," your child replies. "What were you so worried about?"*
>
> *"What do you mean, what was I so worried about? I thought you were in an accident or hurt or sick—"*
>
> *"Or mugged or raped or run over by a steamroller. I'm not a baby. It's not my fault if you get so worried about every little thing."*

You can see that this exchange is destined to escalate into an argument because the child refuses to accept her mother's feelings. Look what would have happened, however, if the child had done otherwise upon coming home late:

"Where have you been?" you scream. "I've been worried sick about you!"

"I'm sorry. I know how worried you must have been. But there was a big accident on the freeway and they weren't letting any traffic through. That's why I couldn't call or anything."

"I thought you were hurt or sick or—"

"I know. You must have been so worried wondering if I was okay."

"I'll say. But thank goodness you're safe and sound."

You can see that this exchange is heading for hot chocolate and pleasant dreams—all because the child defused the situation when she accepted her mother's feelings. Note that the child may have thought that her mother was being silly or overreactive—but that's beside the point. The child could accept her parent's feelings without having to deny her own.

Now reverse the situation. Imagine how your child feels when she says, "I'm scared" (or embarrassed or angry or depressed) and is told: "Don't be silly. You shouldn't feel that way."

Accepting a child's feelings is critical to developing a positive relationship with her. It is not for us to judge and control our child's emotions. Surely we have enough trouble controlling our own. If *Live and let live* means anything, it means keeping our paws off our child's feelings. This unconditional acceptance is enhanced when you . . .

Use Reflective Listening Skills

The use of these techniques helps a child to feel understood and valued. This is especially important in recovering families where children have learned to hide their thoughts and feelings. Such children will need to rebuild trust in the safety of their environment if they are to risk exposing themselves again. (See chapter 13 for a full discussion of these skills.)

Spend Time with Your Child

Recently, I conducted a survey in which I asked three hundred children if they would like to spend more time with their family. Seventy-four percent of the fifth and sixth graders said, "Yes!" as did fifty percent of the eighth and ninth graders. The time a parent spends with a child is a very direct way of communicating acceptance. It says: "I like you"; "I enjoy your company"; "I value you as a human being."

Look at Things from Your Child's Perspective

Children's thoughts and feelings should not be judged by adult standards. Kids live in a different world. As a recovering father put it, "I think of acceptance as empathy. I try to place myself inside my kid's head, to see things from his point of view. If I wouldn't want to hear what I'm about to say, I shut up."

Reveal Yourself to Your Child

Talk about your feelings and ideas. Let your kids in on your plans and dreams. When you give of yourself, you let your children know that they are worth giving to.

Don't Tease Your Child

Humor is an essential ingredient in family life. Too often, however, such humor takes the form of teasing or sarcasm. A child's looks, body, mannerisms, interests, or escapades become running jokes. The child may even laugh or take up the mantra himself to deflect some of the hurt he feels inside.

Teasing a child keeps the focus on something about which the child is sensitive or the parent is intolerant. Both interfere with the child's ability to accept himself. Sarcasm should be avoided because it is an emotionally dishonest form of communication.

Support Your Child's Interests and Accomplishments

"When I was a kid," said a recovering father, "I always had this feeling that there were certain interests that were parent 'approved' and others that were not. I used to sneak magazines into the house—not of naked women but of cars, because being interested in cars wasn't an 'approved' interest. You'd think my parents would have been pleased that I was interested in so many things. But the feeling I got was that I was interested in all the wrong things."

While it's natural for parents to want their children to share their interests, does it really matter whether a child is interested in science or poetry, animals or airplanes? Whether he plays trumpet or guitar? Or tries out for basketball or ballet? What's important is that children find their own passions and be allowed to pursue them without fear of judgment or ridicule. A recovering mother put it well: "I have to remember that my children are not me."

Support your child's activities and interests: Encourage experimentation, express curiosity, arrange for lessons, pay for half, offer to drive, supply materials. Recognize that it is in the nature of children to be quixotic and dilettantish. Don't be upset if today's passion gets discarded in the dustheap of tomorrow's dream. As you support your children's interests and accomplishments . . .

Be Cautious about Praising Your Child

"What?" Parents are shocked when I tell them that praise can be harmful to their kids. "But, but, but . . ." they sputter, "isn't praise what builds self-esteem?"

No, acceptance builds self-esteem.

"But doesn't praise make kids feel good?"

Yes, and that's why it should be used with caution. Praise leads kids to look for external approval rather than to develop their own powers of evaluation. You see this when kids go to school. In an environment built upon praise and criticism (and reward and punishment), kids quickly learn the benefits of parroting what the teacher wants. The child who challenges the prevailing view may be labeled disruptive and disrespectful. In such an environment, creativity withers. Imagine how impoverished the histories of art, music, and science would have been if great artists and inventors had sought the "A" of approval rather than followed their own instincts.

Praise can also be harmful because, often, parents contaminate it with criticism:

"Your room looks beautiful. *It's about time you cleaned it up.*"

"What a great report card! *You see what you can do when you apply yourself?*"

"Don't you look nice. *I didn't recognize you.*"

Contained within these praising words, like a razor blade hidden in a piece of candy, is a sharp put-down. It's as if the praise is motivated by the parent's expectation of bad behavior. What the child hears is this: "How wonderful that you're not being your usual lazy, careless, stupid self."

Another reason for being cautious about praise is that much of the praise parents offer is an insincere reflex: "Oh, that's sooo beautiful!" says a mother as she looks at her daughter's smudgy drawing (and holds it upside down!); "This is super!" says a father as he barely glances at his child's story. The child may know that what she has done is not great or beautiful and will be confused or hurt by her parent's insincerity. Alternately, the child may be thrilled with her work, only to have her pride undone by "constructive criticism."

Praise leads a child to seek conformity, to measure success in terms of product rather than process, to feel valuable only if valued, to ask, "What do you think?" rather than, "What do I think?"

Fortunately, you can give your child something much more valuable than praise: encouragement. Encouragement fosters self-confidence, creativity, and independence. It leads a child to develop powers of judgment and criticism, to become internally motivated, to work to make herself, rather than others, proud. Of course, there's nothing wrong with parents being proud of their child or with the child wanting her parents to be proud. But parental pride should be a by-product rather than a goal of the child's accomplishments.

There are a number of ways you can use encouragement to convey the type of acceptance that motivates children to want to be their best selves:

- *Notice good behavior, but don't "grade" it.* Praise usually sounds like a verbal report card:

   "What an excellent paper!"
   "You did a perfect job."
   "What a good little boy you are."

   Praise bestows "stars" and "smiley faces." The value of the child's accomplishment is found in the parent's judgment. Encouragement, however, teaches the child to discern for herself the value of her behavior by its consequences:

   "Your father was thrilled to come home and discover that you washed the car."

   "Your baby-sitting was a great help to me this afternoon."

   Comments such as these lead the child to conclude: *I must be a competent person to have been so helpful; it feels good to know that I made my father happy.* Thus, good behavior is motivated not by external kudos, but by internal ones.

- *Ask questions.* Kids often come to their parents in search of praise. They hold out a drawing and ask: "How's this?" Some kids even furnish a negative evaluation as a form of protection—"This is stupid, isn't it?"—and hope to be contradicted.

   In such circumstances you'll be tempted to say, "It's great!" or "I love it!" If you do, your child will be pleased and will probably trot off to make another in pursuit of *Praise II: The Sequel*. But all he has learned from this exchange is that Mommy loves what he did.

When your child comes in search of applause, instead of offering praise, offer your interest and involvement. Instead of telling him what *you* think, ask him to tell you what *he* thinks. Respond to his effort. Shift the focus from your evaluation to his.

"My goodness," you might say, "you've certainly been hard at work all afternoon. Tell me all about your painting." Ask questions. Share your observations. Your responsiveness will be reward in itself. Say: "Look at all those dots!" "What bright colors!" "I see so many interesting shapes." From comments such as these your child will come up with his own evaluation of himself and his skills: *I must be a pretty hardworking kid; I really know how to choose neat colors.* Now, when he goes to do another painting, his head will be ringing with ideas about the painting he just made and the new one he wants to make. And he will be making it, not because you praised him, but because you stimulated his internal motivation.

Having said all this about the pitfalls of praise, I would now like to soften my position a bit. I have painted this extreme picture of praise's dangers in order to shake up your thinking. It is important for parents to understand that kids live in a world in which they are constantly being graded and judged—both formally and informally—by teachers, neighbors, employers, and friends. Television, advertising, and the entertainment industry are even more insidious in dishing out "report cards": All they have to do is present images of "sexiness," "masculinity," and "femininity"; lists of what's "in" and what's "out"; distorted yardsticks of looks, status, and success—and kids will grade themselves!

This external evaluation is so prevalent that it threatens the development of the child's wisdom, creativity, and values. To the extent that parental praise also discourages the growth of these faculties, it is harmful to the child.

So where does this leave us? Well, unless you're a robot, you're going to praise your child. It is a spontaneous, warm, loving response. Children of recovering parents in particular may have been starved for positive feedback during much of their childhood. These kids need to hear that they're smart, kind, thoughtful, competent, and responsible. And you, as a recovering parent seeking to rebuild relationships, will feel a special need to communicate your love and approval.

So, go ahead and say, "Great catch," and "Beautiful job," and "You look so handsome," and "I'm very proud of you." But as you do so, listen carefully to your words. Tune in to the interaction from your child's perspective. Does your child come to you for *the* opinion or *an* opinion? Does your child feel free to challenge your evaluation? Do you see evidence of a creative, independent spirit in your child, or does your child tiptoe around lest others find fault with his ideas?

If your child is confident and assertive, if he knows what he likes, if he is comfortable in his identity and interests, it is unlikely that praise will do him any harm.

If, however, your child is insecure about his worth, if he is tentative about his opinions, if he is afraid to act without being "preapproved," he needs encouragement, not praise. Encouragement to do what he believes is best, to follow his own instincts, to trust his own critical judgment. He needs you to help him learn to say: "*I* think that's great"; "*I* like what I did"; "*I* believe I made a good decision."

Helping Children to Accept Themselves and Others

It is normal for preschoolers to go through a stage in which they seek to order the entire world according to their own rules. During this period kids can be extremely rigid about how and when things are done. They will correct their parents if the sequence of a ritual is altered, if Mommy forgets that the milk has to go in the Big Bird cup. They will get upset if dolls and teddy bears are not in the *exact positions they must go in.* They will tell parents and playmates where they are supposed to stand, how they are supposed to act, what they are supposed to say. One would not characterize this as a *Live and let live* philosophy of life. It is, however, a natural phase that reflects the child's growing awareness of her power to influence people, places, and things. A child this age derives a sense of security from knowing "the way things are." Change threatens this feeling of security, and the child must act to protect the status quo.

As the child grows, this rigid nonacceptance usually fades. The child learns that she must share, that she must sometimes do what others want, and that she is not the only person in the universe (ah, such a traumatic lesson for us all!). The child's siblings, peers, and school experiences reinforce these messages.

Contained within these positive messages of socialization, however, are messages of nonacceptance and prejudice. You can support your child against the forces of intolerance by practicing the following principles:

Set a Good Example

As always, the example you set is your most powerful tool for influencing your child's attitudes and behavior. When you accept your child, when you *Live and let her live,* you accomplish two things:

1. You show your child how to be accepting.
2. You foster your child's self-acceptance.

Self-acceptance is the foundation of other-acceptance. Your child has to be tolerant of herself if she is to be tolerant of others. To encourage your child to be tolerant, you must first conduct a searching and fearless inventory of your own prejudices. Rid your actions and speech of intolerance. Addiction is a great leveler. The friendships we forge in recovery make a mockery of the prejudices we used to hold. We come to accept and respect people whose race, religion, ethnicity, social status, and sexual orientation we used to vilify. We recognize that when we are intolerant, we not only harm others, we harm ourselves.

Talk to your children about intolerance. Your children will see it at school, on the playground, and in social situations with their friends. Use examples from the day's headlines. Help your kids to realize that intolerance isn't always the dramatic extinction of a population, bombing of a building, or desecration of a cemetery. Ask them for examples from their own lives: the kid who's teased because he speaks with an accent, the overweight girl everyone makes fun of, the child with AIDS whose family had to move to a different neighborhood.

Younger children may repeat derogatory words and racial/ethnic slurs they hear. If your child should do this, first ask him if he knows what the offending word means. Often he will not. If this is the case, tell your child what it means. Then explain why it is not a word he should use. Rather than say it's a "bad" word, place the word in the larger context of your family's values:

"We don't use that word in this family because it hurts people's feelings. Calling someone a _____ means you think _____ are bad people. We don't think that way. We think all people are equal no matter where they come from, or what the color of their skin is, or . . ."

Discrimination and bigotry are difficult concepts for young children to understand. Try to use concrete examples from your child's life when discussing these abstractions. For example, you might talk about family friends who would be hurt by such slurs or a time the child himself was teased or bullied.

With adolescents it is possible to discuss concepts of tolerance and acceptance directly. You can ask your kids:

"Why do you think people get so upset over the race/religion/sexual orientation of someone they don't even know?"

"How would you feel if the head of the Ku Klux Klan moved in next door? Would it be all right to throw a rock through his window?"

"Why do you think people are afraid of people who are different from them?"

"Have you ever seen an example of discrimination?"

"Have you ever been discriminated against?"

"Are there any things it's okay to be prejudiced against?"

Don't proselytize. Let your child express her opinions and feelings. State your own values and beliefs. Keep in mind that the natural clannishness of adolescents tends to promote social exclusiveness rather than inclusiveness. Adolescence can also be a time of fear and insecurity for many children, and these emotions breed intolerance. When you accept your child, you nourish her courage and confidence. These traits will promote tolerance.

Teach Your Child the Serenity Prayer

Even if your youngster is the *Live and let live* poster child, there are going to be times when his tolerance is severely tested—by teachers who make his life miserable, by politicians who send his blood pressure rising, by the kid in geography who picks his nose and eats the boogers.

At times such as these your child needs to say the Serenity Prayer. Teach your child the usefulness of looking at the people and events of his life in terms of what he can and can't change. When we live and let live, we aren't really extending some great largesse. We're simply acknowledging reality. It makes sense to let others live their lives, because that's what they're going to do anyway. So why drive oneself crazy with anger and indignation?

Part Three

A Power Greater Than Ourselves

15

Through Prayer and Meditation
The Role of Spirituality in Child Raising

Virtually all addicts come to ascribe their recovery to a power greater than themselves. For some, this Higher Power is God. For others, it is the love and fellowship of a support group, a sense of oneness with the universe, a faith that life has meaning and purpose beyond their awareness. This "God stuff" triggers a lot of discomfort and confusion, and many of us continue to have difficulty with the spiritual aspects of our program long into recovery. No matter what our relationship to a Higher Power may be, we cannot escape one glaring fact: Willpower was never enough to overcome our addiction. Something *out there*—some power greater than ourselves—accomplished what we were unable to do over years, if not decades, of struggle. This raises a number of questions for the recovering parent:

- Can a Higher Power do for me and my children what we have been unable to do for ourselves?
- Will a spiritual awakening make me a better parent?
- Should I encourage my children to believe in a Higher Power?
- What child-raising issues are best turned over to God?
- What is the role of prayer and spirituality in parenting?

Some parents may consider these questions and be filled with scorn and anger, particularly if they are having difficulty with the spiritual side of their program. They will remind us of the tragic stories we've heard about parents who watch their child die while praying for his cure—and never once taking him to the doctor. They will scoff that while we ask God to improve our child's grades, they'll get their child a tutor.

This skepticism and discomfort are understandable. We may be afraid to turn our will and our lives over to some*one—something—*else (although that's exactly what we did for years with our addictions). We may not trust God. We may blame God for our troubles. We may feel that if God knew what we were like, God wouldn't want to get involved with us anyway.

We may confuse spirituality with religion and believe that having a relationship with a Higher Power means we have to become religious. Many of us turned away from organized religion years ago. This may be because we were raised to fear the Almighty: "God doesn't like bad little boys who lie"; "If you're not good, God won't take you into heaven." We may have attended religious schools that taught us that we were wretched and sinful. We came to think of God as angry and vengeful. We hated God for making our lives so miserable. As we got older, we saw the hypocrisy of organized religion and were disgusted by it: the piety that masked greed, intolerance, and spitefulness; the slaughter and evil carried out in the name of the Almighty.

It took a long time for many of us to realize that recovery isn't about religion. It is about spirituality. It is about building a relationship with God *as we understand Him.* Or Her. Or It. Or Them.

Before we can use our spirituality to become better parents, we need to understand more about what spirituality is.

Spirituality is the state of our soul. It is our sense of purpose and meaning in life, our center, our self, our contact with that which lies beyond self. Spirituality is what fills our heart and mind. The meaning of spirituality is different for each individual, for each person's spirit reflects the unique nature of her relationship to self, to others, to the universe, and to God. Thus, our spirituality can be made up of hope or despair, love or hate, life or death. It is something we shape and are shaped by.

When we were using, it wasn't that we had no spirituality. Rather, our spirit was sick. It was poisoned with destructive energies and emotions. Addiction was our spiritual core.

When we focus on our spiritual growth, we become better parents. In fact, numerous studies associate what I call "negative spirituality traits" in parents (e.g., anger, abusiveness, authoritarianism) with social, emotional, and behavioral problems in children. Likewise, numerous studies associate "positive spirituality traits" in parents (e.g., respect, acceptance, warmth) with positive outcomes in children. Thus, one of the best ways to become a better parent is to focus on your own spiritual growth.

How to Grow Spiritually

If we think of spirituality as the essence of our connectedness to self, to others, to the universe, and to God, we can grow spiritually by working to improve each of these relationships.

These relationships, like all relationships, can grow quickly, slowly, comfortably, clumsily, consciously, unconsciously. But the one common denominator they all share is that they grow incrementally. We have to fine-tune them, adjust our expectations.

Prayer is the name we give to building a relationship with God. Meditation is the name we give to building a relationship with ourselves. The serenity we find is what allows us to build relationships with others. When we are serene, we have the courage to endure. We have a sanctuary from fear, resentment, and self-pity.

Let's look at prayer and meditation as ways of growing spiritually and see how they apply to child raising.

Prayer

As long as kids climb trees and drive cars, there will be parents praying in every home. The word *prayer* is laden with emotional content. We can't help but have a gut reaction when we hear it. Depending on the associations we bring to the concept, we may picture pajama-clad children on their knees beside the bed. We may think prayer is fine for everyone else, but "leave me out of it." We may think it's total hogwash, a crutch for spineless people who can't get through life on their own two feet.

You have already built, and will continue to build, your own concept of, and relationship to, a Higher Power. The role prayer plays in your life is a personal matter for you to explore. It is not my intention to make a sales pitch for prayer. What I would like to do, however, is to describe ways in which prayer has helped other parents to build better relationships with their children.

"I always thought of praying as something for 'sissies,'" said a recovering father. "You know, real men don't eat quiche or pray. Meanwhile, my family was going to hell in a handbasket. So one night at a meeting, I was dumping my woes on the assembled masses. Afterward, a friend who knew me well said, 'Are you praying?' *What an obnoxious question,* I thought.

"'Look,' he said. 'I know there's more chance of my being struck by lightning than there is of you praying, but let me ask this. Supposing one of your kids got cancer, God forbid. You would do every single thing under the sun to help him. You'd seek out every doctor, every treatment, every healer, every magic potion—you'd crawl to the other side of the earth if you thought there was even a one-in-a-million chance it would help. So you've got these family problems. And you go to your shrinks, and you go to your meetings, and you read your books. But you don't pray. Even though people you know and respect swear that it has changed their lives. But you won't even try it. Kind of makes you wonder, doesn't it?'

"Well, it's always annoying when someone shines the truth in your face. I tried to rationalize it away. But I couldn't get what he said out of my mind. More and more it seemed really stupid *not* to try praying. I mean, what did I have to lose? Some pride?

"I knew that I could never get down on my knees or go to church. So what I did—and I know you'll laugh—is, on the way to work, I'd pick up the car phone and talk into it. You know, God on the line. That way it didn't look strange that I was jabbering away to no one. I just talked about what was bothering me. Things I wanted to change. Things I was worried about.

"And I'll be damned if things didn't start to get better. There were some mornings when I couldn't get to the car fast enough to make that call. Even now, the skeptic in me wants to say, well, maybe the therapy took hold, or maybe the time I spent talking to my Higher Power helped me to get my head together, you know, explain it in some nice, rational, scientific, twentieth-century way. But you know how they say, 'If it works, don't fix it?' I say, 'If it works, don't ask why.'"

Many of us come to prayer in the manner of this father—out of desperation or with a chip on our shoulder—saying, "I guess I might as well try it. What do I have to lose?"

Well, as it turns out, we have a lot to lose. We lose our anxiety and self-centeredness, our fear, our sense of isolation and mistrust. We slowly begin to experience serenity. It is this serenity that permits us to be loving and helpful toward our kids. Why?

Have you ever watched one of those emergency-rescue shows on TV? As often as not, the people dialing 911 are hysterical. And while they have every right to be, you want to scream, "Calm down! You're never going to help anybody if you don't get a grip!"

When we stray too far from serenity, we get hysterical. We block out reason and action with irrational thinking, projection, and fear. At such times we need to grab hold, to make a connection to a power greater than ourselves. On rescue shows, that power is the 911 operator whose calm competence helps the caller to be strong and to have faith. In our own lives that power is God. And we don't even need an emergency to get God on the line.

Perfectionists want to be sure they're praying "right." They're going to be awfully frustrated, though, because there is no right way to pray. For one parent, prayer is "calling" God on the car phone. For another, it is kneeling in church. For another, it is writing in a diary every night. Some prayers are for guidance, others for forgiveness; some for help, some for thanks. Prayers can be our own words or the words of others.

"I don't know if I pray the way most people think of it," one parent told me. "I just share things that are on my mind with God. I mean, that's how you build a relationship, isn't it? By talking and sharing?"

Yes. And by listening.

Meditation

If prayer is speaking to our Higher Power, meditating is listening. For many of us, meditating is even harder than praying. This makes sense. It's easier to talk than to listen. But we rarely learn as much from talking as we do from listening.

We may resist meditating because we're "too busy" or because we find it hard to secure a quiet place. We may avoid meditating because we fear being alone with ourselves. We use the stimulation and distraction of others to distance ourselves from our deepest thoughts and feelings. Whatever the source of our resistance, it is important that we overcome it. Prayer alone is not enough to build a relationship with God. It would be like trying to build a relationship with someone to whom we only talk and never listen.

Virtually all seekers of spiritual growth meditate. As with prayer, the form this takes can vary widely from person to person. We can focus on our breathing, repeat a mantra, imagine a place of great stillness and beauty, listen to sounds of wind or water, visualize a locus of energy caressing and restoring our body.

Talk to friends who meditate. Read some books. You'll find the method that works best for you. At first, as with all new skills, you may feel awkward, perhaps even silly. Unwanted thoughts will ricochet inside your head. Mental static will drown out any brief moments of serenity. Gradually, however, with practice, you will not only calm your spiritual agitation but come to treasure these relaxing, refreshing moments of solace.

Some recovering parents choose not to meditate in the classic sense of the term. Instead, they practice more personal forms of stillness-seeking. For example, they may begin each day by reading from a book of affirmations, meditating *upon* the message, and drawing inspiration from it.

Other parents may take a walk in the woods each day, jog around the lake at sunrise, practice yoga, play music, or swim seventy laps. They find in these more "active" forms of meditation the same serenity and loss of self-consciousness that others find through more traditional forms.

Meditating cleanses us of the negativity that creeps into our spirit. It opens us up to our Higher Power. When we meditate, we are able to hear God's response to our prayers.

A considerable body of research demonstrates the value of meditation. Studies have shown that individuals can lower their blood pressure and stress levels by meditating. Meditating induces alpha waves in the brain, which are associated with states of tranquillity and relaxation. One interesting study surveyed the frequency of alcohol consumption among a group of 126 adults who began practicing Transcendental Meditation versus a matched control group of adults who did not meditate. Over the duration of the study, alcohol use among subjects who meditated dropped significantly; there was no change among subjects in the control group.[13]

The difference in alcohol consumption between the two groups is highly significant. Among the interpretations we can make is that alcohol and serenity work against each other. This is not to say that a drink isn't "relaxing" to many people. But rather, that the relaxation achieved through meditating is of a different order. It is deeper and purer. Viewed in that context, alcohol is a pollutant of spiritual peace. If, as this study suggests, meditating can induce people to stop drinking, imagine what it can do for people who have already stopped drinking.

Prayer and meditation—talking and listening to our Higher Power—lead us to serenity and a better relationship with ourselves. When we are serene, we are able to hear what our children tell us. We are able to work toward our dreams with patience and humility. Serenity is the soil from which positive spirituality grows. When our Higher Power is there for us, we can be there for our children.

You Are Your Child's Higher Power

While no self-respecting two-year-old ever turns her will over to your care, she certainly turns her life over to your care. You are a benevolent "God" when you provide her with love, food, toys, and adventure. And you are a "mean God" when you send her to bed, take something away, or say No. You are her Higher Power.

She even uses you in much the same way that you use your Higher Power. Picture a toddler at play. She stays close to you, hugs your leg, commands your attention, and then ventures off to explore. Then she comes back for refueling—to be sure you're still there, that you still love her. As she becomes more capable of holding an image of you in her mind and heart, she becomes more independent. Your strength becomes her strength.

In no way am I suggesting that you consider yourself your child's God. (Lord knows we don't need any encouragement in that direction!) But in thinking about the type of parent you want to be for your child, think about the type of Higher Power you want for yourself. Use that image to help guide your behavior as a parent. The Higher Power in whom you confide listens without judgment. The Higher Power that helps you to find acceptance, courage, and serenity is supportive and warm, not scolding and harsh. The Higher Power that helps you to be responsible and honest is trusting, not suspicious; patient, not brusque. Be that kind of Higher Power for your child.

Helping Children to Develop Positive Spirituality

In many ways children embody a deep, positive spirituality the day they are born. When they nurse or bask in the warm security of their father's arms; when they believe in Santa Claus and tooth fairies; when they splash in puddles, burrow into leaf piles, bury themselves in sand; when they are, simply, children, they are alive with spirituality.

We know this is true because it is in relation to our children that we touch *our* most spiritual selves: when we feel the handiwork of God in the miracle of our child's birth; when we are alone in the heart of the night, a tiny mouth suckling at our breast; when we feel the air quiver with our child's raw intelligence; when our world turns upside down if the phone rings at 3:00 A.M.—at times such as these we have grasped spirituality.

As children grow, their spirituality comes under attack. The values and institutions of society are, if not overtly antispiritual, certainly aspiritual. The possessors of money, status, and power are fearful of the nonmaterial. Hypocrisy is threatened by truth, workaholism by serenity, self-seeking by connectedness. Spirituality makes many people uncomfortable; they see it as suspect, frivolous, "New Age" touchy-feely. The only time the power structure embraces spirituality is when it's a high concept for a Hollywood movie. Into this societal spiritual vacuum have come the religious charlatans, faith stealers who count their spirituality in dollar bills.

Our children may come to doubt the value of spiritual growth. Some of this happens naturally as their powers of self-awareness, abstraction, and introspection grow. They wonder about their place in the universe, about God, about their friendships and family bonds, their longings and sexuality. This is healthy; this *is* spiritual growth. It becomes unhealthy, though, when the child's natural spirituality is suffocated by the pressures of getting A's, getting into college, getting a job—getting, getting, getting.

As parents, we needn't so much nourish our child's spirituality as protect it from assault. We need to create an environment that values spirituality, models spirituality, and provides our child with access to the love, solitude, and wonder that help spirituality grow. We can do this in a number of ways.

Beware Religion

Now that I have your attention, keep in mind that religion and spirituality are two different things. One can be religious without having a healthy spiritual life; one can have a healthy spiritual life without being religious; and one can be both religious and spiritual—healthily or unhealthily so.

Many parents wish to raise their child within the traditions and teachings of a given religion. Whether this experience proves spiritually enhancing or not varies with the precepts of the religion, the values and practices of the particular church or synagogue attended, and the personalities of the adults into whose care children are entrusted.

As you make or reassess these important decisions, imagine the experience from your child's perspective. What message does your child get if you tell him how important religion is and then, while he's suffocating inside some stuffy church on a glorious Sunday morning, sneezing his head off because the lady next to him OD'd on perfume, you're home washing the car? Does it enhance your child's spirituality to listen to some pedant drone on for an hour about sinfulness? Will your child develop positive feelings toward God if God's agents on earth are more interested in building religious coffers than spiritual connections?

For me, and most of my elementary-school friends, religion meant having to go to yet *another* school! (As if one weren't bad enough.) Three times a week. More books, more assignments, more tests. ("Sorry, Dad. I flunked Burning Bush.") The only thing that made Sunday school bearable was the excitement spent anticipating our plan to rendezvous in the boys' bathroom at a pre-arranged hour, where one of us invariably got depantsed. After playing hooky as long as we dared, we returned to our classrooms and our Thou Shalt Nots.

The adults who prepared us for confirmations and bar mitzvahs were, by and large, grim and humorless. Whether they were born this way or grew to become this way from a lifetime of dealing with kids who didn't want to deal with them, I do not know. What I do know is that they inspired fear. Religion became another forum for chastisement and failure.

Before you think that I have any sort of bias against organized religion (who, me?), I want to make it clear that there are many congregations today that exude healthy spirituality. They *live* the words they preach. They sponsor creative, caring programs designed to meet the interests and attention spans of children; they are peopled by dedicated, wholesome individuals who share their vision of a loving and tolerant God; they reach out to their communities with compassion and generosity; they focus on what is good in human nature rather than what is bad.

You can get a sense of the spiritual quality of a given religious environment by asking a number of questions:

- What are the teachers like? Are they caring and warm? Do they have an understanding of child development? Do they have personal agendas they bring into the classroom?
- How is the material taught? Is there a focus on competition, grades, and homework, or on cooperation and individual growth? Is the curriculum dull, static, and textbook based, or flexible and alive? Are assignments developmentally appropriate? Are a variety of teaching and learning strategies employed (music, dance, plays, art, group projects, hands-on activities, and so on)?
- Is the thrust of the school one of religious indoctrination or spiritual enhancement? Are kids encouraged to think or parrot?
- Is there a hidden curriculum of bigotry or intolerance for the beliefs of others?

- Are children ever made to feel that they, their gender, or their bodies are bad, sinful, inferior, or shameful?
- Are school personnel responsive to parental questions and concerns? Are parents free to visit, work as aides, and join in appropriate classroom events?

These questions can help to point you toward those religious environments that can reinforce your child's spiritual growth. Keep in mind, however, that religious belief cannot be forced down anyone's throat. If your child is resistant, try to identify the source of his resistance. It may be as simple as not wanting to miss his favorite early morning cartoons on TV (tape them). It may be that your child doesn't get along with his religious-school teacher. It may be a social problem with other kids. Or it may be, for older kids, a fundamental disagreement with the religious doctrines being taught.

While it is natural for those of us who practice a particular religion to want our children to do so as well, our acceptance of our children needs to be total. If, for whatever reason, after we have communicated our feelings and listened to theirs, they do not practice or enter our faith, we must accept that. It is best for us and best for their spiritual growth.

Encourage Prayer

Share with your children the role prayer plays in your own life. Suggest that they find their own way of talking to God—not because you make them (God doesn't like it when parents force their kids to pray!), but because it is something they will enjoy, something that will make them feel good, confident, and safe.

For preschoolers, prayer can be a bedtime ritual. Prayers of thanks help young children to build empathy, gratitude, and a feeling of security. Prayers for "things" are trickier. On the one hand, you don't want to tell your child what he can and can't pray for. On the other hand, children who ask God for Nintendos and Nikes are either, if they receive such bounties, going to be encouraged to ask for more or, if they don't, going to be angry with God. Try to divert such supplications. Suggest to your children that they use prayer time to thank God, to talk to God about things on their mind, to ask God questions—but that they bring their material requests to you.

Prayer can also be a dinnertime ritual. Many families observe a moment of silence rather than a spoken prayer. This approach is a sensitive compromise for families with adolescent children who may feel embarrassed, resentful, or co-opted if they have to participate in a spoken prayer. A moment of silence imposes no constraints on each family member's thoughts, yet allows the entire family to share in the power of silence.

Keeping a diary is another approach to prayer. Older children in particular, who may go through periods of self-consciousness about praying, often find journal-keeping a wonderful way to stay in touch with their Higher Power. After all, God knows how to read.

Encourage Play

When children play, they connect to the world around them. They talk to themselves, to their toys, to each other. They expand and transcend their physical, emotional, and intellectual boundaries.

Support your child's play by (1) valuing it, (2) seeing that your child has time for it, and (3) providing your child with a safe, stimulating environment in which to do it. Imagination endows the mundane with the magical. Sticks become swords, blankets become flying carpets. Toys, dolls, blocks, tubes, cartons—the list of objects children play with is endless. Much of the world isn't safe for children to explore on their own. Help them to create a rich, varied world that is.

Encourage a Love of Music

One *plays* a musical instrument. The choice of words cannot be accidental. Whether your child listens or performs, music takes her into and out of herself. It is a way of expressing that which cannot be put into words, of experiencing emotions and transformations. It has the power to take us back to a melancholy space and time, the power to fill us with buoyancy and energy, the power to unite us with others in soaring orchestral harmony.

Expose your child to music. Let her try different instruments. If she is receptive, encourage her to take lessons. Look for a good fit between your child and the instrument you or she chooses. Be flexible. Kids often try several different instruments before finding one they like and have a talent for.

Encourage Reading

The soothing, rhythmic quality of a parent's soft voice swaddles children in security. It doesn't even matter if the words have no meaning yet. Read to your child. New books. Old books. The same book—over and over and over again. Young children find security in knowing what will happen, in reuniting with their book-land friends. The characters in books are alive for children—Curious George, Madeline, Peter Rabbit—aren't they still *our* friends decades after we first met them?

Books tickle the imagination; they cause children to ask and answer questions. They bring the world and the beyond world into the child's mind, heart, and soul. Stories of distant lands and heroic lives—such is the stuff of which children's dreams and spirituality are made.

Encourage Connections to Nature

Nature fills us with awe and wonderment. It is a power greater than ourselves. Many of us are now able to recognize the natural world as the source of our earliest spiritual experiences: We recall fields of fireflies on humid summer nights and thunderstorms that took us beyond terror; we recall floating with the clouds on a windy fall day and chasing butterflies till we collapsed dizzy on the warm earth, our head spinning, the world spinning, earth, sky, body, soul—all boundaries erased; we watched columns of ants building their world and knew that we were being watched ourselves; we chased falling stars to the wall at the edge of the universe—and climbed over it.

It was at moments such as these that we first experienced a sense of our place in the universe, a transcendence of body, a breathtaking appreciation of beauty, an awareness of the vastness and inexplicability of the cosmos.

Help your children have these moments. Take walks. Aimless, whimsical, spontaneous walks, walks across a field, through a woods, around a pond. It doesn't matter if you can't tell a woodchuck from a woodpile. Let your child set the pace. If you spend an hour going fifty feet, that's wonderful. Imagine how much your child will have seen and felt in that hour, those fifty feet.

Sleep under the stars. Take moonlit strolls along a beach. Skinny-dip in a cool mountain lake. Watch a calf being born. Look at the world upside down through your legs. Rub petals between your fingers. Rescue earthworms after a rain.

Help your child to appreciate all living creatures, to see their interconnectedness. Point out that the rotten, crummy rain that canceled the trip to the beach is causing the duck and crocus communities to rejoice.

Earth is not a toy for human beings. It is a sacred gift—a gift we have abused and dishonored. Make recycling and environmental sensitivity a family value.

If your child wishes to study nature, to know the names and calls of birds, to recognize wildflowers, to learn wilderness survival skills, by all means support these interests. But to support your child's spiritual growth all you need do is encourage your child to notice, appreciate, and protect the natural world.

Encourage Meditation

Children can be taught how to meditate as a way of coping with stress, recharging their batteries, and nourishing their spirituality.

In the school I directed, we offered meditation as a "sports" option. It was quite a sight to see thirty kids laid out on their backs, breathing deeply, sweet smiles stealing across their faces as they traveled to serene and secret spaces. Invariably, the snores of a few who traveled a little too far could be heard by the end of the session.

You may want to meditate together as a family. While it is important to some parents that they be physically alone when meditating, many parents find that they can achieve spiritual aloneness in the company of others. If this is true for you, meditating with your children can be a wonderful way of sharing your spiritual selves.

Encourage Questions

A child asking, "Why?" is a child growing spiritually. Encourage your kids to wonder and speculate. Many of their questions will be unanswerable:

"Does God go to the bathroom?"
"Why did Grandma die?"
"How come God made the earthquake?"
"Where do babies come from?"

Yikes! These are the questions we love and hate. You can handle them, though, if you keep a few thoughts in mind:

- *Keep your answer appropriate to your child's age and level of understanding.* There's the old joke about the five-year-old who wanted to know where he came from. Thirty minutes later, at the conclusion of his mother's carefully rehearsed mini-course on reproduction, the startled little boy says, "No, I mean *where?* Tommy says he's from Ohio. Where did I come from?"

  "Chicago, dear."

  Try to figure out what your child is really asking. A six-year-old who asks, "Why did God let all those people die?" is really asking: "Are you going to die?" Your child is not seeking a theological-philosophical discussion, but a reassurance that he won't be alone in the world.

- *Don't expect to be able to answer your child's questions.* Children ask questions whose answers have defied the greatest minds in history. It is not the answer that nurtures spiritual growth, but the *asking.* If your answer encourages your child to ask more questions, to seek more answers, it is a good answer. This means listening to your child and affirming the importance of his question. Ask your child what *he* thinks. His speculations, once voiced, may satisfy him, and they will also give you more clues as to what it is he really wants to know.

  In responding to your child's questions, use realities he understands. According to the famous Swiss psychologist Jean Piaget, children are unable to think abstractly until they reach a stage of cognitive development known as *formal operations.* This occurs around puberty. Thus, concepts such as the soul, faith, and immortality are beyond the understanding of most children under the age of twelve. If you avoid platitudes and moral simplicities ("It's God's will"; "Bad people get punished") and stick to terms relevant to your child's world, you'll be much more likely to provide the answer he seeks and encourage further seeking.

Encourage Community

Anything that promotes community is spiritual in nature. Think of the times your family spends together as a form of community in which you share and build your love, aspirations, and memories. See if your kids would like to create a family scrapbook. Let them interview grandparents and other relatives to construct an oral family history. They can use a tape recorder or camcorder. Someday these records will be priceless to them as a source of continuity to all that has come before and all that will come to be.

Encourage your children to join their spirits with the spirits of others: to play on school teams, sing in choirs, volunteer at a nursing home, build a clubhouse with friends.

The only antidote to bigotry and divisiveness is community. Community grows from positive spirituality. It grows when people are more concerned with giving than getting, when they mesh their goals and hopes with those of others in order to work together to improve all their lives.

This community is built step by step out of the daily moments of life. Most people's spiritual experiences are not made of lightning bolts and levitations, but of ordinary moments—moments made special by noticing them, appreciating them, sharing them, and becoming aware of the miracle contained within each and every one.

As we nourish the spiritual growth of our children, we can easily become a bit too zealous. (Beware the convert!) We need to remember that child raising is a program of attraction rather than promotion. If we present a model of healthy spirituality and share the means and nature of our quest in appropriate ways, our children will want what we have.

16

Letting Go
Breaking Free from the Mind-Sets
That Paralyze Our Parenting

Letting go is a sane, spiritually rewarding way for addicts to move forward and feel better. No wonder we resist it! Our keep-it-complicated inertia says, *Why travel sprightly through life when we can slog stoop shouldered?*

When we don't let go, we become prisoners of our own making, dragging hurt, anger, and regret behind us like so many balls and chains. We become mired in old habits and indecision. We freeze out hope and the opportunity for growth.

I asked some children of recovering parents what they thought it meant to *Let go and let God.* "It means let God take care of you," said a thirteen-year-old boy.

"Oh, sure," the skeptics among us say, "let God take care of my Visa bill. And while he's at it, maybe he could find me a job, pay my child support, and whip something up for dinner!"

God doesn't cook. Or do windows. But God does take care of us—when we let him.

For parents, letting go is many things: It is trust and forgiveness. It is knowing when we are beating our head against a wall of our own making. It is allowing our children's lives to unfold in their own way in their own time. It is being willing to change and grow along with, and sometimes in spite of, our children.

"I'll never forget the moment I first felt what it meant to surrender," said a recovering parent. "I was in treatment. I had spent years in denial fighting with my family and friends. I was really fighting with myself, trying to rationalize all the destruction in my life. I remember how much energy that took. There was a part of me that wanted to say, 'All right, you win. I'm an alcoholic. Help me,' but I couldn't. That would be like an admission of guilt—that I had been wrong all those years. So, all through treatment I kept resisting. Until one day, call it Higher Power or whatever, I felt this incredible lifting. It was so much more than just a physical feeling; it was as if my soul was being transfused; I didn't have to fight anymore. All the rage and guilt flew out of me and I started to cry— and cry and cry. I think the chaplain set a record for tissues handed out in fifteen minutes' time. I was crying because, for the first time in twenty years, I felt hope. It was that simple."

Surrender is not defeat. It is letting go of the struggle. If you've ever been caught in an undertow, you know what this means. When you panic and try to swim against the powerful currents dragging you out to sea, you quickly become exhausted. Like the alcoholic struggling against a force he cannot conquer, you will drown. If, however, you surrender to your powerlessness, if you let the current pull you where it will, if you work with it rather than against it, if you drift and float and move parallel to the shore, you will soon be free of the undertow's deadly grip and be able to make your way to safety.

When we let go of the struggle, we make our way to safety. And, like the drowning man whose flailings threaten those who rescue him, we, in our surrender, make the sea a safer place for our friends and loved ones.

Letting go does not, however, mean letting go of our responsibilities. It simply means letting go of our torture. This is often a difficult distinction for parents to make.

"Eric is on the verge of failing eighth grade," a recovering mother told me. "Yesterday he said that if he flunks, he's going to drop out of school. My sponsor told me I had to let it go. It was out of my hands. How can I just stand by and let him fail?"

"Can you take his tests for him?" I asked.

"No."

"Can you force him to concentrate? Or to be interested? Or to study?"

"No."

"Have you talked to his teachers?"

"Yes."

"Have you had him tested for learning differences or attention-deficit disorders?"

"Yes."

"Have you had his vision checked?"

"Yes."

"Have you tried tutoring or therapy?"

"He refuses to do it."

"All right, then. You've done everything you can do."

"But what if he flunks anyway?"

"I know that that seems like the worst thing that could happen. But it's such a narrow focus. Let's say he does flunk. At that point you face a new set of options. Maybe he could go to summer school and pull it out of the hat. Maybe he should go to a different school. Maybe he stays behind a grade and becomes the star pupil of his class and his self-image improves."

"Maybe he drops out of school," muttered Eric's mother.

"Maybe he does. But is your faith in him and his future, or in your Higher Power's plan for him, so limited that you can say that his failing eighth grade would be the end of the world? And even if he does drop out of school, where is it written that he can't go back? I'm not knocking the importance of an education, believe me, but he's only fourteen. Are there things he cares about? Let him go live on a farm school for a year. Send him to school at sea. Let him fetch coffee and doughnuts for that filmmaker you know. Maybe he'll become a great director, or maybe he'll get such a taste of the 'real world' that he'll hightail it back to the sanctuary of school."

"That's easy for you to say."

"I know. But you have to let go of the things you can't control. Otherwise you're just beating your head against the wall, which doesn't help your son at all."

Understandably, Eric's mother was focused solely on her son's schooling. She approached the issue as if school were the only route a child could take to personal and professional success—and as if that route allowed for no detours or altered timetables. Granted, school is the traditional route to "success"; it is the easier route. But it is not the be-all and end-all of a child's life. In fact, Eric was probably picking up an unintended message from his mother that his worth was measured in terms of his report card. Her lack of faith would soon become his. If Eric's mother could let go of her self-imposed, self-limiting assumptions, the situation would take on hues of possibility and hope:

> *I would prefer that Eric not fail but if it happens, it is not my fault. While I do not wish my son to be hurt or embarrassed, he may learn valuable lessons from this experience. I have seen him work hard and show interest in life, and those traits will stand him in good stead. My faith in his abilities and good character will also be of help. Together we will consider the options—which will be many and varied.*

This perspective on Eric's situation changes the problem from an expressway to doom into a meandering route into the unknown, from a locking of horns into a merging of concerns.

When we let go, we open ourselves to feelings of loneliness and uncertainty. We test our faith in ourselves, our children, and our Higher Power. We confront an unknown future without the illusion of control we had built so carefully over the years.

In letting go we must confront lost years, irretrievable relationships, missed opportunities. There may be words we wish we could take back, actions we wish we could undo. We must, in turning away from drinking and drugging, say good-bye to what was often the "best friend" we ever had and to many of the people and places that went with it. If we have not let go of these things, we are stuck somewhere along the process of grieving: stuck in shock, denial, despair, guilt, or anger. Only after moving through these emotions and letting go can we accept that the past happened and move on from there.

Let Go of Guilt and Shame

Most of us in recovery feel terrible pain when we recall the effects of our addictions on our children and family life. We may have abused, ignored, or overindulged our children. There is nothing we can do to change that. What we can do is take an inventory of our wrongdoings. We can reincarnate the guilt or shame we feel into the courage and motivation we will need to become better parents today.

Let Go of Worry

Worry is the most useless emotion ever invented. It is mental self-mutilation. We worry all week about whether it's going to rain on our yard sale, whether our kids will turn to drugs, or become pregnant, or do poorly on their SATs.

"I think of my children as in God's hands," said a recovering mother of three. "Sometimes I use this to let go of late-night worries about them."

Worry eats away at our faith in ourselves, our children, and our Higher Power. If worrying suggests a responsible action that can be taken to protect or help a child, fine, take the action. But let go of the worry.

Let Go of Projection

Most of the fear we feel as parents comes not from reality but from imagined scenarios. From the tiniest acorns of possibility we grow whole oak trees of dire predictions: A failed multiplication test places our child's entire future in jeopardy; a charge of vandalism predicts a life of crime and incarceration. If worry is stewing in what *might* happen, projection is living in what *will* happen. And since it usually *doesn't* happen, projection is make-believe. It is the creation of a phantom world in which we relate to our children not on the basis of what is but on the basis of what isn't.

"Letting go," said a recovering father of two teenagers, "keeps the projecting that I do for myself and for my kids to more manageable proportions. I can't solve everything—in fact, as it happens, I can't solve much. So I don't try to predict what will or what won't happen. I have a hard enough time dealing with what does happen."

Let Go of Hurts, Grudges, and Labels

In the same way that we have to let go of self-recriminations, we have to let go of any grudges we hold toward others. We have to allow our children to make their own changes as we make ours. Nothing will be gained from scorekeeping, from "I did this but you did two of that." The slate must be wiped clean. It is time to let go of family lies, myths, and stereotypes. It is time to deal in reality.

Let Go of the Need to Control Your Children

The best reason for letting go of the need to control your children is because you can't control them. "I don't understand what you mean," a parent once said to me. "When I make my child clean up his room, or do his homework, or wait for me in the car, isn't that control?"

No, it is not. In every case, it is the child who is controlling himself. You're not *making* him do anything. The child chooses to clean up his room. The child chooses whether to stay in the car or not. Unless a parent ties her child up or subjects him to a reign of emotional torture, there is nothing she can do to directly control the child's behavior. There are, however, all sorts of things parents can do to encourage their child to want to *control himself.* Punitive parents do this by issuing threats, inspiring fear, offering bribes, and handing out severe punishments. These methods may work in the short term, but in the long term they prevent the child from developing her own self-discipline and moral awareness. Parents who are warm and nurturing, however, encourage their child to want to control herself. They notice and reward good behavior (rather than seek out and punish bad). They model the values they hope their child will adopt (rather than say one thing and do another). They help their child to anticipate and experience the consequences of her actions (rather than issue "Because I said so" dictums for her conduct).

This approach encourages the child to think about how her behavior affects others. It encourages her to consider the type of person she wants to be and the type of values she wants to embrace.

Let Go of Unreasonable Expectations

It is not your child's job to fulfill your expectations. You may want her to be valedictorian, captain of the swim team, or president of her class. You may want her to play the piano and love to read. You may want her to be artistic, extroverted, sociable, and married with three kids and a high-paying job by the time she's thirty. Let go of these expectations. They are not hers; they are yours.

Once you let go of these controlling expectations, a new set will fill their place. Wish for your child to be honest and trustworthy—for these character traits will stand her in good stead. Wish for your child to have the capacity to love and be loved—for this will bring her happiness and growth. Wish for your child to develop her skills and intellect—for this will bring her confidence and opportunity. Wish for your child to be creative and passionate—for this will keep the child in her alive forever. Wish for your child to feel a deep, nourishing spirituality—for this will fill her life with meaning and joy. Your child will feel these wishes not as commands but as votes of confidence.

Let Go of Your Child

There are many points in a child's development when he moves away from his parents: The toddler becomes more willful and independent; the four-year-old goes off to nursery school; the ten-year-old spends the night at a friend's house; the fifteen-year-old locks his door and keeps secrets; the young adult moves out of the house (and, in a few rare instances, no longer looks to his parents for financial support).

Parents view these milestones with pride and delight. Mixed in with these feelings, however, are others: sadness, loneliness, jealousy, rejection. This is natural. Children and parents are bound at the heart; what affects one affects the other. As the child becomes more and more independent, the parents may feel more and more useless, unloved, unappreciated.

Raising children is an ongoing process of letting go. The world of the child is constantly growing; it is the parents' job to ensure that their child is allowed to grow with it.

Parents need to build protective fences around their children. But these fences must be appropriate not to the parents' fears or need to control but to the child's age and development. They must respect the child's need to explore and experiment, for it is only by running and tripping and getting up again that children learn to meet the challenges of life.

Watching one's child range across broader and vaster fields is both joyful and sad for parents. The child's maturing reflects the parents' aging. The child's expanding options highlight the parents' diminishing ones. Letting go is rarely easy. But, as your child pushes for greater freedom and independence, take heart, because it is a sign that you have done your job well.

Helping Your Child to Let Go

Our children will travel through life with greater ease, pleasure, and lightness if they, too, learn when and how to let go. Young children tend to do this naturally. Few two-year-olds are wracked with guilt over the mush they threw at Mommy the week before.

Inevitably, however, as a child's mind evolves, as his self-awareness deepens and his feelings unfold, his capacity for accumulating and holding on to "baggage" increases. You can help to ensure that your child will be enlightened rather than encumbered by his baggage.

Ritualize Good-Byes

Hold a "funeral" for a pet, conduct a good-bye tour of the neighborhood, throw a going-away party for a best friend. Commemorate the past by marking the present. When you do this, be sure to . . .

Encourage Your Child to Express Her Feelings

In our desire to move children out of their pain, we can make the mistake of disallowing them their feelings. We do this when we say:

"The new house will be so much nicer," instead of:
"I know you feel very sad about leaving this house."
or
"You'll make new friends," instead of:
"It's very hard to leave behind such good friends."

Feelings need to be expressed, acknowledged, and accepted before they can be left behind.

Discuss the Concept of Letting Go with Your Children

You will encounter situations in which it is clear that your children are holding on to some disappointment, feeling, or failure from the past. Or they may be eating themselves alive with anxiety over the future. In such cases, talk to your kids about the idea of letting go. This is when the power of self-talk can be used to run stinkin' thinkin' out of town (see chapter 9).

Explain to your kids that life is a journey. As they travel that journey, they accumulate baggage. This baggage can consist of nice, durable suitcases (on rollers!) full of friends, knowledge, good memories, tools for living, and dreams. Or it can consist of huge, unwieldy trunks overstuffed with worry, fear, guilt, resentment, and self-deprecation.

Explain that their journey will take them past all sorts of people and opportunities. Sometimes they will be able to influence the shape of the landscape, sometimes not. Sometimes things will work out to their liking, sometimes not. The idea of letting go is that we don't weigh ourselves down with things from the past that we can't change or things in the future that we can't control. Explain that they can choose the kind of baggage they carry.

Help your kids to relate this construct to the feelings, people, and events they confront. If they're beating themselves up over the past, point them toward amends they might make. If there's nothing they can do, ask them if they'd like to let go of their pain or regret or recrimination. They may be able to do this simply as the result of their new understanding. They may wish to write a letter to themselves or to draw up a "whereas-whereas-therefore-be-it-resolved" contract with themselves in which they formally relinquish the baggage. They may wish to let go in prayer or meditation. They may wish to enlist the help of friends if there is a group dynamic involved.

Help your children to realize that while they can't control the past or the future, they can control how they feel about it. This is the key to letting go.

17

An Attitude of Gratitude
Nourishing Our Appreciation of Our Children

When I was a school headmaster, I participated in hundreds of parent-teacher conferences. There is one that I will never forget.

The Colsons were new to the school. This was our first conference and I had been looking forward to it all day. Dr. Colson was a psychiatrist. I had been impressed by the fact that he only practiced three days a week. "Why work myself to death when we can live comfortably on what I make in three days?" he had explained when we first met. His attitude was so refreshing in an age of rampant workaholism that I had taken an instant liking to him. (I also made a note to look into psychiatry as a career.) His wife was a social worker, and together the two of them came across as relaxed, confident parents.

It was my habit to start a conference with a general description of everything that was wonderful about a child. "What a great kid you've got!" I said. "We're all in love with Amy." I went on to praise this scrappy little kid with the untied sneakers and stand-up smile. Sure, she could be a bit careless in her work and sometimes her spelling left something to be desired, but we'd get to that in due time. Meanwhile, in the things that counted—character, creativity, responsibility—this child was a gem. "I have to tell you one more thing," I said. "We've been having this problem with kids forgetting to do their school chores. So we brought the issue up at a meeting, and Amy came up with this great idea...."

Tears streamed down Mrs. Colson's face.

Oh, great, I thought. "Did I say something to upset you?"

"No," she said, half laughing, half crying. "It's just, listening to you say these things, I'd forgotten what a terrific kid she is. I'm so used to hearing about her terrible handwriting and how she doesn't sit still or get her work in on time, that that's how I'd been thinking of her—in terms of the little things that need fixing and not the big things that don't."

Perhaps some evolutionary force propels us to gloss over the good and seek out the bad in our lives in order to better ourselves and our environment. The addictive personality, however, invariably takes this to an extreme. This is why gratitude must be at the core of our personal programs of recovery.

Gratitude is the antidote to self-will run riot: *I want what I want and I want it now!* While this attitude is perfectly appropriate in a two-year-old, it is not particularly becoming in a forty-two-year-old. Yet most of us never let go of it. If we receive our desired bounty, we take it for granted and move on to the next item on the wish list. Grandiosity and self-seeking are reinforced. And if we don't receive our (perceived) due, then it's poor, pitiful me: *Why does everything go wrong for me? Why is my life so terrible?*

We can't be grateful for what we have because no matter how much it is, it's never enough to fill the void. The void is a spiritual one. It will never be satisfied by things and conditions, by "if onlys."

Ingratitude feeds addiction. It keeps us focused on problems rather than possibilities, obstacles rather than opportunities. The cup is always half empty—so we are always half empty. Ingratitude is a prescription for eternal spiritual unrest.

Gratitude, however, keeps a lid on our egos. When we are grateful, we are focused on others. We cannot be grateful and selfish at the same time. We cannot be grateful and self-pitying at the same time. Gratitude opens the heart and unleashes generosity and tolerance.

As parents, we must make gratitude an active force for the benefit of the entire family. We must communicate our gratitude to our children: gratitude for what is good in our lives and gratitude for what is good in them and their lives. If we fail to do so, we turn our relationships sour and risk introducing into our family's soul the spiritual malaise we once felt in our own.

There are four principal ways in which one-day-at-a-time parents can use gratitude to strengthen the spiritual health of their children and family:

1. Model gratitude for your children.
2. Nurture within yourself the gratitude you feel for your children.
3. Communicate your gratitude.
4. Encourage your children to use gratitude as a positive force in their own lives.

Let's look at each of these aspects of family gratitude in greater detail.

Model Gratitude for Your Children

Children learn best from example. Let your child see how you use gratitude in your own life to maintain serenity and perspective. You can do this in a number of ways:

Share Your Gratitude List

I know one recovering mother who keeps her list on a scroll of parchment that, I swear, must be a hundred feet long. I don't know that I've ever seen her without it. It is her talisman. I can just picture her in a white robe at the breakfast table, recently down from the mountain, unrolling her scroll, reading to her kids: "I am grateful for my new job. I am grateful for my health today. I am grateful for the beauty of Scrubwillow Pond, which I see every day on the way to work. I am grateful—"

"Hey, Mom, I'd be grateful if you'd pass the milk!"

Act Grateful

It's important to remember that gratitude is not just a list. Gratitude is action. If you feel financially blessed, give money to charity. If you feel blessed with good health and energy, volunteer your vitality so that others may benefit from your time and skill. If you feel blessed by the wondrous beauty of nature, support environmental causes. Make the linkage between your gratitude and your behavior explicit for your kids: "I'm so grateful for my sobriety that I want to do everything I can to help others to become sober."

Let Your Children in on Your Grateful Thinking

One of the ways we use gratitude is to maintain emotional balance in the face of hardship or disappointment. You can offer your kids a valuable lesson on keeping things in perspective if you lift the curtain on your thoughts and let them peek inside.

A single mother I know recently lost her job when the company she worked for went belly up without any warning. She had no severance pay; her accumulated vacation leave was lost; and she would soon lose her family health insurance. Her biggest concern, apart from finding a new job, was how and what to tell her two children who were in their early teens. We groused and commiserated and bemoaned the sorry state of the world, yet came no closer to solving her problem. "If I tell them how I really feel," she said, "it's going to worry and scare them." We sat in silence for a while. I kept coming up empty-handed in my search for the magic words of comfort. "Oh, well," she sighed, "at least it didn't happen when I was still drinking."

"Hark," I teased, "is that gratitude I see before me?"

And suddenly, the solution was before us. In the midst of this unexpected crisis there was much for this mother to be grateful for: She was clean and sober; she would qualify for unemployment compensation; she had enough savings to keep the wolf from the door for about four months; she had decided several weeks earlier not to buy a new car that would have obligated her to a large monthly payment; she had excellent references and a network of contacts in her field.

Gratitude had opened the door to a solution. Now she knew what she would say to her kids: "I've lost my job. It's pretty scary. But even with this bad news there's a lot I have to be thankful for." And she would go on—not as Pollyanna but as a realistic, mature adult—to detail all the things for which she was grateful. In counting their blessings, she and her kids would feel comforted, and a framework for action would be built.

This is one of the most important lessons we can teach our children: Gratitude leads to action. When we are grateful, we are focused on our assets and skills. We marshal our troops: inner strength, friends, family, experience, knowledge, sobriety. When we are ungrateful, we are focused on impossibilities, on what we don't have. We generate fear and self-pity rather than courage and hope. Gratitude anchors us in today, and today is where all action begins.

Nurture within Yourself the Gratitude You Feel for Your Children

Take a cross section through your family. What do you see? Are your kids healthy and strong? Are they moral and affectionate? Do you enjoy your time together and communicate intimately and easily? Do you and your spouse have a comfortable relationship and division of parenting? If you're one of the three parents in America who can answer yes to all these questions, you are indeed fortunate.

Let's say, however, that you're like most parents. Mixed in with the good is the not-so-good. Conflict and estrangement. Anger, pain, and mistrust. You and your spouse get at each other's throat. One child does poorly in school; the eldest just totaled the car—drunk. At times such as these gratitude doesn't come quite so easily. But there is still so much to be grateful for if only you look. You can be grateful that you are still together as a family, that your son wasn't hurt in the accident, that you are clean and sober. You can be grateful that you never hit your children, that they have good teachers in school, that your youngest child excels at sports, that your sensitive, artistic eldest—if he is headed down the tunnel of alcoholism—can benefit from your wake-up call.

This doesn't mean that you isolate yourself in a cocoon of gratitude and turn your back on the problems. For example, your youngest child's interest in sports offers an arena in which you and she can develop your relationship. Practice with her. Take her to games. Take her teammates out for ice cream after a match.

You were grateful for the quality of your child's teachers. This is another opportunity for action. Make an appointment to talk to them. Find out what they see. Discuss your family and your recovery as you feel is appropriate. See what you can do together for your child.

No matter how bad things are, no matter how troubled the cross section of your family, there is always something for which you can be grateful. Use that gratitude to point the way toward progress.

Communicate Your Gratitude

When we were focused on the negative in our lives, we made ourselves pretty miserable. Yet this is precisely what many parents do with their kids.

I'm reminded of a parent who sent two children through my school. One afternoon she came early for car pool and plunked herself down in my office. Her eldest son, Hugh, had left us the year before and was now in public high school. He was every parent's dream: handsome, personable, intelligent, motivated, responsible. He had come back to visit us recently and had told me that he was captain of his high school tennis team, treasurer of his class, and "acing" all his courses.

"I don't know what to do about Hugh," his mother said.

"Why? What's wrong?" I asked.

"He just doesn't practice," she said with a tone so full of venom and disappointment, you'd have thought she was describing her son the teenage mutant serial killer.

"Practice what?"

"Guitar. He wanted music lessons and we gave them to him and now he doesn't practice."

"At all?"

"Well, he practices, but nowhere near enough."

"Does he enjoy it?"

"He loves it. He's formed a band with some friends—"

"So what's the problem?"

"The problem," she said, obviously exasperated at the density of my gray matter, "is that if he's going to take lessons, he should practice. There's no point doing it if he's not going to work at it."

The bell rang and Hugh's mother left to round up her charges. Rather than be grateful for all that was wonderful in her son, Hugh's mother took it for granted; it was, after all, what she expected from her children. Her radar was tuned to fault finding, and in her son's less-than-heroic commitment to practicing, she found it. This is ingratitude.

Hugh eventually gave up his lessons. It was preferable to the ongoing struggle with his mother.

If we only notice our children's lapses, that will be all that they will notice. This can be avoided if we remain focused on what is good in our children. One-day-at-a-time parents do this every day in a number of ways.

Tell Your Child That You Are Grateful

We lecture our kids on their faults. How many of us lecture them on their virtues?

"I can't just sit down and tell my kid I think he's great," said one father. "It would embarrass both of us." Many parents have expressed this feeling to me. To them, I respond: "Try it. The worst that can happen is your child will blush and run off feeling wonderful."

You can also use context to support your expression of gratitude. If your child has just helped her younger sibling in a thoughtful, caring way, you can say: "I'm so grateful for the way you played with your sister this afternoon. It gave me some time by myself, which I really needed." If your child comes home from school all fired up about a project to help war orphans, you can say: "I feel very lucky to have a child who cares about other people as much as you do." These expressions of gratitude will not only feel less awkward for the parent but will mean more to the child than abstractions out of the blue.

Thank Your Children for the Little Everyday Things They Do

You fill many roles simply because you are a parent: chauffeur, cook, banker, launderer, homework helper, nurse, referee. These obligations come with the territory. Even so, it's nice to be appreciated. There are times when you'll feel taken for granted, when your children or spouse will exude a sense of entitlement. At these times, nothing is more welcome than a thank-you from your family for the little things you do for them, whether a ride to soccer practice, a stack of clean laundry, or a plate of warm cookies.

Children, too, should have age-appropriate obligations simply because they belong to the family unit: baby-sitting, washing the dishes, cleaning their rooms, and so on. In some households, parents also use their children as the "downstairs" staff: *Be a dear and go get my glasses; run and turn off the kettle; go tell your father I need to ask him something.*

Just because kids should have responsibilities doesn't mean they shouldn't be thanked for doing them. Such gratitude will help you to appreciate them and them to appreciate you.

Lead with Your Gratitude

When you must correct your child or point out some error or misdeed, gratitude is your best approach. Start with what is good, right, and well done. Perhaps you asked your child to clean up his room. An hour later you go to inspect and see a mess of toys, clothes, and papers remaining in one corner. A typical parent might say: "I thought you said you were finished. Is this what you call cleaning your room?" Immediately, the child feels ashamed, angry, afraid to respond with what may be a logical explanation. A one-day-at-a-time parent would lead with her gratitude: "This looks so much better. I can see all the work you've done. Thank you for cleaning it up so quickly. What do you plan to do about those things in the corner?"

This approach treats the child with warmth, dignity, and respect. It encourages him to admit his lapse: "Oops, I forgot about them" or to offer an explanation: "I ran out of space to put them away"; "They're Billy's things and I didn't know what to do with them." When gratitude leads the way, solutions usually follow.

Keep in mind that this type of gratitude is not meant as a sneaky disguise for chewing your kids out. Its purpose is to put your kids' imperfections in perspective—for both you and them. Make sure you communicate pure 100 percent gratitude on many other occasions. Otherwise, your children might think: *Uh-oh. Mom just said something nice. That means she's going to tell me I did something wrong.*

Encourage Your Children to Use Gratitude as a Positive Force in Their Own Lives

Many children, of course, come by their gratitude easily. They have been blessed with good parents, good circumstances, and good values. Children of alcoholics, however, may not feel very grateful, particularly if their dependent parent is in early recovery.

It may be some time before your children are on speaking terms with gratitude. You can, however, facilitate the likelihood of this happening in a number of ways.

Recognize That Gratitude Cannot Be Forced

Gratitude is like respect. You can get your kids to mouth it, but you can't make them feel it. The feeling can only come from within. Never say to your child: "You should appreciate everything you have." These expressions give gratitude a bad name by turning it into a weapon of shame.

Don't Belittle Your Child's Feelings by Projecting Her Gratitude for Her

In our own lives, we often use gratitude when we have just had a major disappointment or setback. We use it to keep our wits about us, to control our ego, to maintain balance. But *we* are the ones using it and feeling it. Someone else is not telling us to do so. Imagine how you would feel if you lost your job, or your house burned to the ground, or your spouse left you and a friend said, "Well, you should be grateful it wasn't worse," or "You weren't getting along all that well with your wife anyway."

You might very well come to these conclusions yourself—in your own time. But it's galling when somebody else barges into the middle of your crisis and tells you what you should feel.

The traumas of childhood are many: breaking up with a boyfriend, making the error that lost the game, not being invited to a party, having a friend move away, living with an alcoholic parent. At times like these your child needs your love. She needs you to hear and accept the depth of her pain. Tempting as it may be, do not offer gratitude as a salve; do not tell the child who broke up with her boyfriend: "Be grateful you had such a nice time at the prom," or the child who lived with an alcoholic parent: "Be grateful I'm in recovery." Responses such as these belittle what your child is feeling at that moment.

Later, when time and empathy have helped your child to get over her hurt, you can introduce gratitude as a tool she can use by herself to feel better in similar situations in the future. Here's how.

Share Your Own Experience

Relate an incident from *your* past in which gratitude helped you to recover from a great disappointment. Be sure to begin with a statement of empathy. Ask your child how she's feeling about whatever happened. Whether she's still down in the dumps or climbing out of the doldrums, you can commiserate:

"I know how sad you must feel. I remember I had a boyfriend in eighth grade, Jimmy Waterman, and he was the cutest guy in the whole class—at least I thought so."

"Oh, Mom!"

"We went together for the whole year, and then, two weeks before the end of school, we broke up. I cried so much, you could have filled an ocean with my tears. So that summer, instead of spending every second with Jimmy like I had planned, I found I had a lot of free time. That's when I started to take pictures and fell in love with photography. So, if I hadn't broken up with Jimmy, I might never have become a photographer. I also met some new kids who lived nearby that I hadn't even noticed before. We became very close friends. Later, I realized that none of this would have happened if I had still been going with Jimmy. It was strange to think that some good things had come from something that seemed so bad. So when I'm hurt or disappointed, I let myself feel that way, but I also try to look for the good, because that helps me to get over the hurt."

This type of gentle sharing can help your child to look for the good when she's surrounded by the "bad." There are several other things you and your family can do on a daily basis to promote gratitude:

Play the Gratitude Game

One person proposes a real or made-up "bad" scenario. For example, a hurricane wipes out a town in Florida; aliens visit Earth and abscond with the entire population of New York City; a member of the opposing team accidentally pulls your basketball shorts down during the championship game.

Once a scenario is proposed, the other players have to find the "good"—something for which one could be grateful. For example, the hurricane eroded a beach and a treasure-filled galleon was discovered and everyone in the town ended up ten times richer than before; when your shorts were pulled down, the other team was so distracted by your beautiful body that your team made the winning basket!

This game can be lots of fun. Wild suggestions should be encouraged; the more imaginative your kids become in looking for the good, the more likely they will be to find it in their own lives.

Keep a Gratitude Page in the Family Logbook

Invite your kids to join you in jotting down grateful thoughts. The thoughts can be about each other, about the world, about the day. Be sure your kids know that it's great to feel gratitude toward themselves: *I'm grateful that I do well in school; I'm grateful that I don't have a pimple the size of a tomato on my nose!*

When enough thoughts have accumulated, read the list aloud so that all can share in each person's gratitude.

Write Thank-You Notes

Thank your kids for their gifts and smiles, their thoughtfulness and sparkle. Thank them for all they bring to your life. They'll catch on and start writing thank-you notes to you. You can have even more fun by placing your notes in unexpected or silly spots where you know they'll be found: inside a sock, in a tub of ice cream (better wrap it in foil first), stuck to the ceiling in your child's bedroom, and so on.

Encourage Your Kids to Express Gratitude in Bedtime Prayers or Dinnertime Grace

If your children say bedtime prayers, you can suggest that they include people, events, and things for which they are grateful. The same theme can be introduced into spoken grace at dinner. Remember, though, no statement of gratitude should ever be ridiculed or challenged.

The ideas in this chapter will help you to nourish your own gratitude as well as your children's. One last thought: Gratitude should be fun! Some of the activities presented here are meant to be silly and playful. One reason gratitude often "annoys" people is because the concept is presented with such piety—as if the only thing we should feel is perpetual gratitude. When we or our children get knocked flat by the winds of life, we should allow ourselves to feel sad, disappointed, and hurt. We should grumble and hang our heads. That's natural and healthy. Then we should search for the good, balance our perspective, muster our courage, and let gratitude show us the way out.

Part Four

It Works
If You Work It

18

Our Common Welfare
Nurturing the Fellowship of the Family

Family unity can only be achieved collectively. One father learned this the hard way:

"I approached my family's recovery the same way I approached everything when I was drinking—I was going to tell everybody how to 'get well.' I had read a lot of the codependency books, so I thought I knew just what my 'enabling' wife and kids needed to do. And I knew the importance of honesty and communication and spending time together, so I commanded that we would be honest and communicate and spend time together. Needless to say, my family was in no mood to have me tell them how and when to get better. It was like rubbing salt in their wounds."

Family healing cannot be dictated. In many ways it is like happiness: You can wish for it, but you can't will it to happen. It is a by-product of attitude and activity. Fortunately, there are a number of things you can do to promote the type of attitudes and activities from which family unity flows.

Make a Family Commitment to Getting Better

Many families avoid discussing the tasks and traumas of healing that lie ahead, as if doing so were just as taboo as talking about addiction used to be. This is a mistake. Recognize the new "elephant in the living room": family recovery. Say to your kids, in words appropriate to their age:

"My addiction created a lot of problems for this family. It caused a great deal of hurt for individual family members. It interfered with our ability to work together as a family, to grow close, and to support each other's interests and goals. We learned to hide our feelings, opinions, and needs. You have every right and reason to feel angry and confused about what happened. There's nothing wrong with you for feeling that way. There are, however, many things we can do to help each other to feel better and to help our whole family to feel better. I'm going to do everything I can to work toward those goals. If you would like to help, too, I know we can become a healthier, happier family."

Most children will be relieved to hear such a statement. It acknowledges their feelings and validates their sanity. They will also be excited about the prospect of finally being able to do something.

Don't Drink, and Go to Meetings

Not *that* kind of meeting. A *family* meeting: a time when parents and children get together to share ideas, make plans, and solve problems. This is the ideal forum for being explicit about family needs, goals, and issues.

You can introduce the idea by explaining to your children that people who share common objectives—be they football players, teachers, co-workers, or members of a family—need to get together to talk about their plans, problems, and concerns. It's how they stay in touch, support individual initiative, and work effectively toward their goals.

The following suggestions will help you to establish family meetings and optimize their value:

- *Meet regularly.* Find a time once a week when all family members are free. This time should be sacred and come before all other priorities. (If an unavoidable conflict prevents a family member from being present, try to reschedule. Never reschedule for conflicts that are frivolous or avoidable.)

- *Invite but do not demand attendance.* Most children will be curious about family meetings and will want to come. If, however, any of your children are hostile to the idea, accept this without recrimination. Make it clear that their participation at any time is welcome and valued but that it is up to them whether they wish to attend or not. If they choose not to, they must realize that decisions that affect them may be made without their input. Be sure you continue to welcome their attendance. This way they'll know that they can change their mind without risking rejection or loss of face.
- *Post an agenda in a conspicuous place.* Encourage your children to join you in writing down items for discussion. While late-breaking issues can always be brought up at the meeting, the agenda allows people to do some thinking ahead of time.
- *Rotate the "chair" among all family members.* The "chair" brings the agenda, runs the meeting, and maintains order. Rotate the position among all family members. This prevents any one person from dominating and is an excellent way to encourage responsibility. (Even children as young as five or six can run a meeting if they have watched it done on several occasions.)
- *Don't meet for too long.* When people get restless, tempers get short and thinking gets sloppy. Generally, the longer the meeting, the less that gets done. It's better to schedule a second meeting than to push on beyond everybody's endurance. Some families schedule agenda items involving younger children first so that they can be excused afterward if they wish.
- *Keep notes.* Many ideas and solutions to problems require follow-up from week to week to see that everything is

going according to plan. Have a scribe take notes at each meeting. The scribe's job is to keep track of decisions, ideas, actions, topics tabled for future meetings, and so on. He or she can also remind people between meetings of any important deadlines or responsibilities. (This position can rotate or, if one family member enjoys doing it, be fixed.)

It is natural for children to place a lot of problems and complaints on the agenda, particularly if they are testing the safety and sincerity of the family-meeting format. Such items may trigger comments and emotions that cause discomfort. While it is important to encourage the open exchange of feelings, you don't want the tone of family meetings to become negative. You don't want your kids to equate *family meeting* with *family fighting.* There are several things you can do to prevent your get-togethers from becoming "gripe-togethers":

- *Talk and listen respectfully.* This is critical to keeping the spirit of family meetings friendly and hopeful. (See chapter 13 for a discussion of positive communication techniques.) At your first meeting, solicit ideas for "rules" people would like to follow. Add your own suggestions until the list looks something like this:

  All talk should be constructive, i.e., aimed at solving rather than blaming.

  No attacks or "You-statements" allowed.

  Don't accuse. Say how you feel. Use "I-statements."

  Listen when someone else talks.

  No labeling of people's ideas as dumb, silly, and so on.

- *Be sure there's always a "fun" item on the agenda.* If your kids don't suggest one, make sure you do. Fun items include

  Getting a dog.

  Planning a camping trip.

Deciding what to do on Mom's birthday.

Brainstorming what to get Grandma for Christmas.

- *Have a "What's New" time.* Set aside a few moments for kids and parents to share what's going on in their lives. This is an excellent way to keep communication open and build empathy for the stresses and challenges individual family members face.

- *End each meeting with a pleasant ritual.* Make a point of closing your family meetings on an upbeat. This could be a game of badminton, a trip to the ice-cream parlor, a boisterous hug, a video rental. The adage "never go to bed angry with your spouse" should be applied to family meetings as well: Never adjourn a family meeting if you're still angry.

Identify and Solve Problems

The common welfare of the family depends on timely problem solving. This doesn't mean that family meetings should be called fourteen times a day. Many problems disappear with time *(This too shall pass)* or with a change in attitude *(Progress not perfection; Live and let live).* If, however, a conflict persists that disrupts relationships and family functioning, then the problem must be addressed.

Problems that demand immediate solutions (e.g., two siblings fighting over who gets the last Popsicle) must be tackled on the spur of the moment. Other less urgent conflicts can be brought to the next family meeting. In either case, the structure for healthy problem solving remains the same:

1. Identify the problem.
2. Brainstorm possible solutions.
3. Evaluate options.
4. Select a plan (and follow through).

As you utilize this approach, the following ground rules will de-personalize conflict and lead to the most effective solutions:

Identify the Problem

Each person states what he or she thinks the problem is. Different people may see the problem in different ways. This is fine as long as statements are made without blaming, accusing, or judging anyone.

Accusations ("You keep hogging the computer and it's not fay-aire!") provoke defensive postures and counter-accusations. Neutral statements ("I would like to be able to have more computer time") encourage cooperation and creative thinking. Sometimes, problem solving is facilitated by framing the issue as broadly as possible. For example, a child may state a problem as, "I need a bigger allowance." Such a definition suggests only one solution: *Cough it up, Dad!* A broader definition, "I would like to have more money," opens up all sorts of options: a bigger allowance, a loan, getting a job, working around the house, holding a yard sale, and so on.

Many parent-child conflicts exist simply because nobody acknowledges them. Parents and kids *allow* them, *perpetuate* them, are *controlled* by them, but rarely call time-out and say: "Hey, we've got a problem. Let's solve it."

Kids like to solve problems. They adore brainteasers. If you try to frame problems as puzzles to solve, you'll be amazed how speedily intractable conflicts can be dismantled and moved out of everybody's way.

Brainstorm Possible Solutions

Once the problem is defined, you're three-quarters of the way toward a solution. The next step is to think of as many ways to solve the problem as you can. You can do this informally in the course of a discussion or more formally at a family meeting with the scribe taking notes. The idea here is quantity, not quality. Wild, uncensored ideas often lead to sound, productive solutions.

In this step, no criticism or commentary is allowed ("It'll never work"; "That's dumb"; "Too expensive"). Brainstorming demands a judgment-free atmosphere if participants are to speak without fear of ridicule or rejection.

Evaluate Options

When no more ideas are forthcoming, it's time to end the brainstorm and move on to the discussion phase of problem solving. Encourage your children to lead the evaluation. Be careful not to allow personalized judgments to creep in at this stage. Ideas can be discussed in terms of cost, feasibility, fairness, responsiveness to the issues involved, likelihood of success, and so on.

Be wary of the tendency to latch on to an unworkable solution just so you can say you've solved the problem: Does the child actually have the income to pay for half of a new phone line? Is it realistic to think computer time can be limited to thirty minutes per child per day?

If a viable solution doesn't present itself, don't panic. Give it some time. You may need to take another look at how you defined the problem. You may need to have another go at brainstorming. You may wish to invite additional participants to join the problem-solving process.

Select a Plan (and Follow Through)

Once you've agreed on a solution, figure out what you need to do to put it in place. Solutions should be the result of consensus. Forced solutions tend to unravel through conscious or subconscious sabotage. If someone is still upset, chances are good that not everyone's needs and feelings have been acknowledged. Some solutions may require compromise or a trial period to test viability. Check at subsequent meetings to see how things are going. If the solution has broken down, it may be necessary to fine-tune the plan, reassign responsibilities, or reassess the problem.

By identifying and solving problems as they come up, you and your children can eliminate those festering conflicts that poison family unity. There are many other things you can do to promote family fellowship:

Keep the Family Logbook

This is a mainstay of communication for many recovering families. It's a place to record goals, wish lists, requests for help, affirmations, reminders, and so on. Its uses are limited only by your family's creativity.

Maintain and Invent Family Rituals

You can promote family fellowship by maintaining and/or creating family rituals that are meaningful to you and your children. Such rituals can include mealtime, bedtime, and birthday traditions; holidays, vacations, recreational activities, television nights, and so on. In fact, research indicates that children who grow up in alcoholic families that maintain family rituals are significantly less likely to exhibit behavioral or emotional problems, or to become alcoholics themselves, than are children who grow up in alcoholic families with disrupted rituals.[14] This is a very important finding for parents in recovery, whose children are at higher risk for becoming substance abusers themselves.

Don't feel bound by the rituals of others. If you want to exhaust yourself with a fourteen-course, twenty-eight-relative Thanksgiving dinner, fine. If, however, you want to celebrate Thanksgiving by serving food at a shelter for the homeless or by taking in a movie and taking out a pizza, that, too, is fine.

Rituals can be small: the tuck-in routine at bedtime, the

thumbs-up sign you give your child when he leaves for school, the surprise dessert you place in a lunch box every day.

Recovering parents speak of all kinds of rituals:

"Each third Saturday of every month a different child gets to plan an all-family activity. The only requirement is that it include everyone and be cleared by the budgetary council—which is me."

"The children's mother died when they were young. Every year we plant a tree on her birthday."

"Once a week we take one hour to blitz the house. We turn the music up loud and vacuum, dust, and straighten things up. Then we make tacos for dinner."

"We go camping every year to celebrate the summer solstice. After dinner, we build a fire and make all sorts of idiotic offerings to the sun god. Poems, dances, mud pies. The kids are getting older and I have the feeling this may be the last year for that ritual."

The last parent on this list raises an important point. Rituals need to change as people change. Obviously, the bedtime ceremony so vital to a four-year-old would be a bit bizarre for a fourteen-year-old. Family vacations and celebrations also need to be reconsidered as children mature and their interests and priorities change. If your kids seem reluctant to participate in certain rituals, seek their help in identifying the source of their hesitation. Sometimes, though, it's simply time to let go of old rituals. But don't worry. As long as there's family fellowship, new ones will soon fill their place.

Choose a Weekly Goal

Family unity can be enhanced by selecting a goal toward which all family members agree to work. Such goals (e.g., keeping the house cleaner, thanking people for the things they do, not watching any TV for a week, getting more exercise) emphasize the idea that "we're a team." Equality of personhood is stressed when Mom and

Dad have to try just as hard as the kids to meet the goal. You can decide at your family meeting if you want to build in a "reward" to motivate effort.

Weekly family goals don't always have to be serious or "productive" either. Their purpose can just be to have fun or try something new: dressing up for dinner, eating vegetarian meals, composing a family anthem, and so on.

With older children you can set family goals that are more distant or abstract such as building a cabin on a family-owned plot of land, giving Mom the support she needs to finish her degree, being more sensitive to other people's feelings, and so on.

Establish a "Command Central" Post

Every family needs a communications center for schedules, reminders, phone numbers, lists of responsibilities, cartoons, photos, and newspaper articles. To create your own "Command Central," hang a bulletin board in a well-trafficked area. You may wish to locate a small blackboard there as well. It can be a child's responsibility to keep the communications station fully stocked with chalk, thumbtacks, notepaper, and pencils. Other items you may wish to keep here could be the family logbook; family meeting agendas; the goal of the week; minutes from family meetings; idea lists for activities, trips, and extra-money jobs around the house; daily inventory sheets.

Assign Chores

For many parents and children, the conflicts that arise from chores are a prime source of family disharmony. This is a shame, for chores, if presented in the proper context, can be a positive component of family life. They can teach children responsibility, foster self-confidence, and instill a sense of belonging.

When should you start assigning chores to your children? The younger the better. Even toddlers can be given tasks to perform. Of course, children this young don't distinguish between work and play; to them, handing Daddy socks from the laundry pile or finding all the raisins on the floor is fun. In fact, children this age love to play with child-sized versions of grown-ups' tools and appliances of drudgery. When your toddler gives you a hand with household responsibilities, let her know that you appreciate her help. Introduce the notion that helping out is part of belonging to a family.

As children get older, they may resist or forget to do their chores. You can minimize the chances of this happening if you keep the following ideas in mind:

- *Appeal to your child's sense of fair play.* Explain to your kids that it takes a lot of work to keep a family and a household going. Discuss the types of jobs and responsibilities that need to get done. Encourage your kids to think of a family as a small business that can thrive only if certain tasks are accomplished. If chores are presented as an important contribution they can make to the success of their family, they are more likely to be cooperative. It's the difference between saying: "I only have one pair of hands!" and saying: "This family really counts on your help."

- *Have a regular family chore time.* Depending on the nature of the tasks involved, establish a daily and/or weekly time when chores are done. Such a time might be fifteen minutes before dinner or each week prior to the family meeting. A ritualized slot emphasizes the fact that all family members have responsibilities and makes it less likely that children will forget their chores or feel unfairly treated.

- *Get your kids involved in identifying and assigning responsibilities.* We all have certain jobs we (a) enjoy, (b) don't mind, and (c) hate! It's silly to insist that a child do a job she loathes if one of her siblings wouldn't mind swapping with her. If you involve your children in the process of negotiating and assigning responsibilities, they will be much more likely to follow through with their responsibilities. And if they don't?

- *Find out what the problem is.* Don't nag. Don't punish. Don't name-call. Instead, say to your child: "I noticed that the trash wasn't taken out last night."

    If your child says, "I forgot," you can ask, "What can we do to help you remember next time?"

    If he says, "I don't see why I have to do it," or "How come I get stuck with all the rotten jobs and Daniel doesn't have to do anything?" you need to approach the issue as a problem to be solved. Perhaps your child is right and the system isn't fair. Perhaps it's time to gather the whole family together to discuss the assignment of chores. In any case, the important thing is to get feelings out in the open, identify the problem, brainstorm for solutions, and put new plans into effect.

    But what if kids still don't do their chores?

- *Let the cookie crumble.* It's time for logical consequences, the parent's best friend. Some parenting experts recommend that the consequences for *not* doing chores be stated to the child up front. They argue that this cuts down on disagreements later. While I see their point, I disagree with this approach on two counts: First, advance warning of what will happen if you drop the ball undermines the positive expectations parents need to communicate to their kids. It's like saying: "Before you even have a chance to show how responsible you are, here's what's going to happen if you aren't!" Give your kids an expectation to live up to, not down to. (The only exception to this would be if your children ask, "What happens if we forget?" In this case ask them, "What do you think should happen?" Let them take the lead in laying out consequences.)

The second reason I object to stating consequences upfront is because it undermines the whole idea of the concept. If a consequence is logical, it flows from a particular action at a particular time occurring for a particular reason and involving a particular person. Each of these factors should rightly influence the nature of the consequence. What's logical for one child may be illogical for another. The response to a chore forgotten in the heat of creative passion might logically be different from the response to a chore willfully ignored in a fit of anger. The consequence for a first-time "offender" might logically be different from that for a repeat offender. How can you possibly figure out in advance fair consequences for the myriad permutations of children, tasks, motivations, and reasons for nonperformance?

When irresponsibility occurs, deal with it. But don't project it before it even happens. (I would also make one additional exception to this advice: If you are entering into a trial period with your child where you are extending a freedom or responsibility about which you have hesitations, you are perfectly justified in asking that the consequences for nonperformance be stipulated in advance. In this case, it is clear that such stipulation is part of what allows the "deal" to go forward.)

Perform Service Work Together

In the same way that individual family members can contribute to the welfare of the family, families can contribute to the welfare of the community in which they live. The benefits of doing so accrue not only to those who are helped but also to those who do the helping.

Discuss with your children some of the ways in which your family could help others, as well as the reasons for doing so. Brainstorm ideas for involvement. Activities could include giving the environment a boost (e.g., joining highway cleanup patrols, organizing recycling programs), becoming active in politics, mentoring, visiting and helping the elderly, and so on. Children who sing or play musical instruments or who like to read aloud are highly prized by nursing homes and other institutions. Many hospitals have active volunteer programs; I know of several that use volunteers to hold and cuddle newborns who do not have caretakers.

Many newspapers feature community bulletin boards that list organizations that welcome volunteers. Your church or synagogue, your place of work, and/or your child's school can also be good sources for ideas.

19

HALT
Taking Care of Our Children by Taking Care of Ourselves

Hungry. Angry. Lonely. Tired. We all feel this way from time to time. So we fix a snack, go for a walk, call up a friend, take a nap. When recovery is going well, we are able to make these minor adjustments to keep our lives moving in healthy directions. Sometimes, however, we get overtaken by events and emotions. We cut back on meetings. We begin to suffocate on the stagnant air of our own company. If we're not careful, if we don't recognize the danger signals, if we don't use the tools we've learned in recovery, this type of self-destructive cycle can lead us straight to relapse.

Hungry. Angry. Lonely. Tired. We recognize these feelings as threats to our serenity and sobriety. But they also threaten our ability to be good parents. If we are not taking care of ourselves, we are not taking care of our children. One way of knowing whether you're taking care of yourself is by asking the following questions:

- Am I impatient and irritable with my children?
- Am I criticizing my kids and taking their inventory?
- Am I bouncing between extremes of indulgence and hostility?
- Am I trying to control my kids' lives and feelings?

- Have I withdrawn from family activities and become self-absorbed in my own issues?
- Do I feel hopeless about my kids' problems or my ability to parent?
- Do I blame my children for my own moods and problems?
- Am I seeking inappropriate support and solace from my children?
- Am I neglecting to provide the minimum essentials of proper child care such as food, clothing, supervision, and medical attention?
- Am I abusing my children emotionally or physically?

If you answered yes to any of these questions, it is a sign that you're not taking care of yourself. Don't expect your family to call you on your behavior and attitudes. They may have their own need to deny that the honeymoon is over or that old problems have returned. They may be scared to death that anything they say will tip you over the brink. They may be focused on their own issues, oblivious to your behavioral Maydays. In any case, they are likely to respond to your "dry drunk" in the same way they responded to your "wet drunk": by shifting roles and responsibilities; masking feelings; adjusting, accommodating, and enabling.

At times like these, you need to stop immediately any abusive behavior toward your family, recenter your life around your program, and marshal your support resources.

How to Take Care of Yourself

You'd be surprised how often we fail to recognize and satisfy our most basic human needs. I am reminded of the recovering mother who complained to me that she felt depressed, had no energy, and could barely stay awake at work. After inquiries into her psyche failed to turn up a cause, I jokingly said, "Well, maybe you need to eat a bigger breakfast."

"Oh, I don't eat breakfast," she replied. Nor, as it turned out, did she eat lunch. Well, you don't need a Nobel prize in nutrition to suspect caloric deficiency as the cause of this mother's fatigue.

And then there was the father who couldn't concentrate. He complained of feeling tense, anxious, and irritable. It never occurred to him that the thirty cups of coffee he drank every day might have something to do with it!

We owe it to our kids to take the best possible care of them. This means taking the best possible care of ourselves—seeing that our physical, emotional, and intellectual needs are met. The following suggestions will help you to do just that.

Get Regular Exercise

The more active you are, the more energy you'll have. With your doctor's approval, exercise strenuously for at least twenty to thirty minutes three or more times a week. Get the ticker pumping, the endorphins flowing! It's a great natural high. Join an aerobics class. Jog, swim, work out at a gym. In addition to its many physical benefits, exercise has been shown to produce feelings of well-being, to reduce depression, to promote sound sleep, and to motivate other health improvements such as balanced eating and the cessation of smoking.

Your chances of following through with an exercise program will be enhanced if you begin at an appropriate level. Don't expect to run the marathon the first day out. Set realistic goals. Choose activities you like. Maintain a regular schedule. Keep records to track your improvement. Invite a friend or child to work out with you. Exercise brings immediate rewards (mixed in with a little soreness too). If you keep at it, you'll quickly reach a point where you won't want to stop.

Take Up a Sport

Play tennis or basketball. Bowl. Golf. Join a softball or soccer team sponsored by your community or place of work. Learn to scuba dive. Feel tired when you get home from work? Challenge the kids to a rousing game of badminton, Ping-Pong, or tag. It'll wake you all up and promote good family feelings (as long as you don't get upset if they win).

Eat Right

Contrary to popular opinion, this does not mean heavy on the chocolates and tortilla chips! A car fueled by the wrong gas, or not fueled at all, doesn't run too well. Same thing applies to human fill-ups. If you're not eating regular, balanced, nutritious meals, you're undermining your recovery and your ability to be a good parent. While there's always at least one new dietary claim making headlines, the basics of healthy eating are pretty well agreed upon in terms of fat and cholesterol consumption and spreading your diet among the four food groups: candy, ice cream, pizza, and nachos. Just kidding. Seriously, consult with your physician and read some books to ensure that your eating habits are appropriate to your age, weight, lifestyle, and medical needs.

Sleep Right

Getting the right amount and the right type of sleep is essential to maintaining good health. Talk with your doctor if you suffer from insomnia, if you sleep excessively, if you feel chronically tired, or if you experience other sleep-related problems.

Monitor Your Health

A young mother I know was recently thrilled to discover that she had a thyroid condition. Why thrilled? Because the utter exhaustion she had been feeling now had a cause. Having assumed that her fatigue was the result of a new baby and moving to a new house (and certainly such activities might drain even the most robust mothers of a bit of energy), she had feared that she might feel this way forever. What a relief, then, to discover that a simple medical solution could take care of the problem.

Follow the recommended guidelines for seeking dental and medical care. Be on the lookout not only for major health problems, but for the low-grade infections, headaches, hormonal deficiencies, toothaches, gum diseases, and so on that can sap your energy and spirit without your even being aware of it.

Maintain Good Hygiene

I don't mean this to sound like a sixth-grade health class lecture, but . . . keep yourself properly toothbrushed, vitamined, combed, and cleaned. When you're depressed, it's common to let your personal-care habits slide. Physical discomfort exacerbates emotional discomfort. Break the cycle by perking up your physical self. Take a long, luxuriant bath. Wash your hair until it squeaks. Get your skin tingling with lotions or aftershave. Put on fresh clothes. You'll feel better.

Keep Your House in Order

Our physical environment is another thing we let slide when we're hungry, angry, lonely, or tired. Pretty soon, our surroundings are as much of a mess as we are. Closed blinds, stale air, unwashed dishes, trash on the floor, dirty clothes, stacks of old newspapers, unemptied ashtrays, and moldy, mutating food do not a happy human make. You're not taking care of yourself if you don't take care of your environment. Your children are also affected by the gloom and filth.

Throw open the curtains. Let the sun pour in. Rinse the house with fresh air. Clean things up—but not everything at once. Nobody can do that. Just pick one small task. Once you've done it, you'll probably feel *more* energetic rather than *less*. Choose another discrete task; keep going until things are clean or you've had enough for the day, whichever comes first.

Do Nothing

There's a big difference between feeling depressed and doing nothing, and feeling serene and doing nothing. One of the worst *musts* we set for ourselves is the one that says, "I must at all times be engaged in making myself richer, smarter, leaner, meaner, and more successful." Baloney! Let's hear it for idleness. Not laziness, procrastination, or sloth. But idleness.

Be still. Watch the clouds float by. Listen to the wind weave through the trees. Nurse a soda at an outdoor cafe. Sit with your eyes closed in the sun (under a heavy coat of no. 15 sunscreen).

Do Something

Engage in active idleness. Take a walk. Go for a canoe ride. Feed the birds. Make a sketch. Take some photographs. Read a book. Pursue a hobby.

When we don't do the things we feel we *should* be doing, we feel guilty. To punish ourselves for not being "productive," we do nothing. The time gets wasted. Look, the time is going to pass no matter what you do. So why not fill it with something you enjoy? You may end up feeling so relaxed and fulfilled that you'll be able to tackle that other project you've been dreading.

Feed Your Mind

Learn new skills. Enroll in a course. Get that diploma. Finish that degree. Take up a musical instrument. Go to a museum, art gallery, play, film, or concert. Many cultural institutions have free admission times; check out matinee and dress rehearsal performances for reduced rates.

Don't deprive yourself of the joy of intellectual growth as an adult just because it may have been spoiled for you as a child.

Plan Your Pleasure

Your calendar should always contain something to which you're looking forward: a sports event, a romantic dinner out, a vacation, an evening with friends. While it's fun to do these things on the spur of the moment, it's easier to get through today's dreariness if you can anticipate tomorrow's bright spots.

Beware of Continuing Addictions and Compulsive Behavior

For most of us in recovery, our primary addiction was our most destructive one, and once we gave it up, our lives and health improved tremendously. We may, however, still have other addictions: nicotine, caffeine, sex, codependent behaviors, and so on. While we can't change all aspects of ourselves overnight, we need to recognize that we may still be suffering from other addictive behaviors that, while perhaps less dramatic or life threatening, continue to harm or limit our lives—and the lives of those around us.

Recovering from our major addiction is a beginning, not an end. If we are to take care of ourselves, we must continue to keep our nose to the grindstone of growth, seeking new ways to improve our spiritual, emotional, and physical well-being. We must do this with *Progress not perfection* as our goal. We must set priorities and ask for help, and remember that *Easy does it* is the way to do it.

Anticipate Stress

Stress is unavoidable. Events, whether trivial or tragic, bring anxiety into our lives. The tension, fear, or grief we feel is a normal response to unpleasantness; the discomfort serves to motivate us to take appropriate action. Stress can also be created by joyful circumstances: promotions, weddings, children going off to college. We want enough stress to keep us sharp, motivated, and growing but not so much as to impede our ability to function and enjoy life.

Sometimes when we are under stress, we get stressed about being stressed. At these times, we need to remind ourselves that stress is natural. It comes and it goes: *This too shall pass.* We need to be gentle with ourselves, to exercise patience, to acknowledge our limits, and to recognize that we are a lot healthier when we confront stress than when we flee from it.

Many of the anxiety-producing events in our lives can be predicted: holidays, exams, deadlines at work. If you were traveling to a part of the world where you'd face a higher-than-normal threat of disease, you would get inoculated for extra protection before leaving. Do the same if you see that you're heading for a place of greater stress. Keep things simple. Focus on your priorities. Let the little stuff slide. Be on the lookout for stinkin' thinkin'. Stay in close touch with your support network. Talk. Ventilate. Ask for help. Take extra good care of your physical health. Watch what you eat. Get the sleep and exercise you need for optimal energy. And most of all . . .

Work Your Program; Go to Meetings

If there's one refrain we hear over and over again in our support groups, it is that taking care of yourself means going to meetings and working your program. When you are under stress, this is the time to lighten your load with an amend, to stay in touch with your sponsor, to do Twelve Step work, to read program literature, to communicate with your Higher Power.

Share the Health

When we take care of ourselves, we strengthen our serenity and sobriety. Helping ourselves, however, needn't be a selfish act. In fact, many parents make taking care of *everybody* a family goal. One recovering father spoke to this:

"When I beat a path through the house for my 'nap,' the family scatter like chickens from a coyote. I know they're thinking: *Let*

Dad have his nap; we could lose everything *here.* They know I have to take care of myself. But they also know that that's so I can take care of them and we can take care of each other."

Of course, you, as parent, bear the ultimate responsibility for taking care of your children. You must see that their emotional, physical, social, and educational needs are met.

At the same time, however, you want to encourage your children to learn to care for themselves, to nourish their own spiritual and physical well-being. Here are some ideas for sharing the health:

Model Taking Care of Oneself

Show your kids how to take care of themselves by showing them how you take care of yourself. This doesn't mean being saintly and preachy, or haranguing them with reminders of the *put-your-hat-on, button-up, did-you-wash-your-hands-brush-your-teeth-and-go-to-the-bathroom* variety. Rather, present a good example for them to follow. With younger kids, you can narrate your self-care so they understand why you're doing it: "Daddy is going to sleep early because he needs extra energy for tomorrow"; "Mommy jogs every morning because it's important to get exercise."

Be Up-Front When You Need to Focus on Yourself

If you have to put a HALT to stinkin' thinkin' or unhealthy personal behaviors, say so. Your kids will support your efforts and learn a valuable lesson for dealing with such circumstances themselves. State the problem and what you're doing about it:

"I went to see a doctor today about my blood pressure. She taught me some things I can do to reduce stress. So, every evening before dinner, I'm going to go into my study and meditate. It would help me a lot if you kids could keep the house quiet during that time. And if you'd like me to teach you what to do when you feel stressed out, let me know."

Use the Family Logbook to Take Care of Each Other

Caretaking needs and behaviors can be made explicit in the family logbook. Start an entry entitled "How I Took Care of Myself Today." Encourage your children to join you in jotting down such items as

Child: I put on my long johns.

Dad: I meditated for fifteen minutes.

Child: I told the teacher after class that I didn't understand least common denominators.

Start another entry for "Things the Family Can Do to Help Me Take Care of Myself." Such listings might include

Child: Stop asking me if I have my schoolbooks every morning.

Teenager: Buy me a sports car so I don't have to bug you for rides. (Ha, ha!)

Mom: Rotate cooking responsibilities so I can have some time to myself.

Since *Asking for help* is a primary means of taking care of ourselves, another listing might be "Things I Need Help With." Such items might be

Child: Fighting with Becky.

Dad: Taking care of the yard.

Mom: Finding my sunglasses.

Child: Feeling sad.

Teenager: This problem at school where Debby told Sean that Billy said I told Diana that I liked Joey Billings but really I like David Warburg but Sean told David what Debby told him and . . .

Conduct Home Safety Inspections

This is a great way for everybody to look out for everybody else. Go through the house or apartment with your kids. Ask them to hunt for safety hazards: overloaded sockets, frayed extension cords, improperly stored flammable agents, loose railings or steps, slippery rugs, lead-based paint, windows little kids could fall out of, poorly vented heaters and furnaces, smoke detectors with dead batteries, and so on. Definitions of what constitutes a hazard will vary with the age of your children—obviously, the younger your kids, the more potential dangers in the environment. Encourage older kids to make the house and yard safer for their younger siblings. Acquaint your kids with what to do in case of fire. Identify emergency exits. Hold fire drills.

Without alarming your children, discuss the possibility that illness or accident might require them to seek help for themselves, a family member, a friend, or even a stranger. Explain to your kids when and how to call 911 for emergency help.

Another excellent family caretaking activity is to enroll in a first-aid course. Classes on CPR and emergency first aid not only teach children how to save a life but also help them gain valuable self-confidence.

Few activities provide greater protection for less effort than putting on a seat belt. If your kids are not already in the habit, it's time that they acquire it. Set the example by buckling up yourself. Let a child be "seat-belt monitor." The car doesn't move until she gives the okay.

Appoint Family Health Monitors

At a family meeting, introduce the idea that every family is a living organism that has health needs very similar to those of its individual members. For example, families have their own social, emotional, and intellectual lives; families have many goals and experiences in common; families often go through periods of stress or loss together; the problem of one family member can quickly become the problem of all.

Brainstorm with your kids a list of habits, activities, and issues that relate to and affect family health; for example, eating, recreation, sleeping, privacy, bathroom habits, money, going to church, dressing right, getting work done, having fun, keeping the house clean.

Don't seek any particular slant for your list—your children's ages and interests will govern the way in which they approach the challenge. Once you've completed your list, ask your kids if they would like to join you in volunteering to monitor family health in one (or more) areas. In other words, one child could become the "Minister of Physical Activity"; her responsibilities would include planning family sports and recreation activities, encouraging and supervising individual exercise programs, suggesting field trips that might enhance motivation or skill building (such as season hockey tickets to inspire outings to the local skating rink). Another child could be the "Minister of Culture," or "Secretary of Stress Reduction," or "Chairperson of the Healthy Eating Committee."

Don't try to become the perfect family. Focus on a few priorities. The point is to have fun, to do things together as a family, and to underscore the importance of healthy living habits. If you run into logistical difficulties or find that individual family members resist group goals, bring the issue to a family meeting.

Talk with Your Children about Drugs and Alcohol

Few factors exert greater influence on a child's ability to take care of himself than his relationship to alcohol and other drugs. Research leaves little doubt that children raised in substance-abusing homes are at increased risk for becoming substance abusers themselves. As a parent in recovery, you need to recognize this risk and to do everything possible to help your children avoid it. This means talking and listening.

It's ironic that a family can be controlled by drugs and alcohol for years without any discussion of drugs and alcohol ever taking place. Kids can grow up surrounded by the wreckage of alcoholism without explicitly recognizing alcohol as its source. Kids in substance-abusing families seem to be torn between two poles: (1) an abhorrence of drinking that pushes them to say: "I'll never drink when I'm grown up!" and (2) a legacy of emotional pain and life-skills dysfunction that propels them toward the very chemical dependence they abhor.

As a parent in recovery, you have certain advantages and disadvantages when it comes to talking with your children about alcohol and other drugs.

Advantages:

- You've been there. You understand the nature of the disease and its progression.
- You know the lies, deceptions, and rationalizations that accompany substance abuse. You're apt to recognize them in your child.
- You understand that you cannot coerce your child's abstinence and/or moderation.

Disadvantages:

- From your child's perspective, you have a credibility problem. Who are you to talk about or advise your child on the dangers of drinking and/or taking other drugs?
- Your own experiences may bias your reading of your child's situation. You may deny your child's drug or alcohol abuse in much the same way that you denied your own. Conversely, you may approach the issue with too much projection and alarm. You may see addiction in experimentation, lasting character defects in the passing traits of adolescence. Be on the alert for feelings or hidden agendas that might impede your ability to talk honestly and rationally with your children.

You can encourage your children toward healthy attitudes and behaviors with regard to alcohol and other drugs in a number of ways.

Establish an Atmosphere of Trust and Openness

For years your children got the message that they weren't allowed to talk about drugs and alcohol. Let them know it's different now. Your kids may be afraid that if they bring up the subject, it might make you use again. Let them know that they needn't worry. They may be afraid that if they tell you the truth about their experiences, you will criticize or punish them. Your reactions over time will show them that this fear is unwarranted.

When you first discuss these issues, it's often best to do so on an impersonal level. Try using events in the news (e.g., drunk driving accidents, drug busts, lawsuits against cigarette companies) to solicit your children's opinions about drinking and driving, drugs in schools, smoking, peer pressure, and so on. Ask them what they think most of their friends would say or do in a given situation, what their friends' attitudes are, what drugs their friends have been exposed to. Often, the answers your children give will be *their* answers—safely disguised by the way in which the question was asked. As you apply program principles to your relationship with your children, your communication with them will become more open and honest, and you will be able to discuss these issues directly.

Role-Play

Children as young as eight or nine years old may find themselves in situations where they are offered alcohol and other drugs at school, on the playground, or at friends' homes. You can help your children to prepare for this eventuality by asking them what they would do in such a situation. Have them role-play with their siblings and friends. Encourage them to come up with as many ways as possible to deal with it. Make sure they realize that it is their *right* to refuse such offers.

Let Your Older Children (Ten and Up) Know That They Are at Higher Risk for Developing Substance-Abuse Problems Themselves

Explain that this may be due to genetic and/or environmental factors. Let them know that they can protect themselves from this possibility by the choices they make. Avoid scare tactics—they know that one drink or joint won't turn them into an addict. Share elements of your "story" that relate to their circumstances—the pressures you felt at their age, the unhealthy things you did, the damage you feel it caused, the denials and deceptions you fell into. Don't preach or lecture. Just share your experience.

Set Limits

With the participation of your spouse and children, establish limits regarding your children's alcohol and other drug use (e.g., drinking at parties, wine at dinner, drug experimentation). You'll need to be realistic in the boundaries you set. For example, a rule for older teenage children—*Absolutely no drinking ever!*—may be so inappropriate in their actual lives that it would beg to be broken. It is far better to set reasonable limits that reflect reality: that is, the laws in your state, the types of social events your children attend, and so on. Many parents have found it effective to draw up contracts that spell out what their child should do in the event that she or someone else driving has been drinking or using other drugs. Such contracts usually stipulate that the child agrees to call home in such circumstances and that the parent, without hassling or lecturing the child at that time, agrees to pick her up, pay for a cab, or make alternate arrangements to guarantee her safety. All participants to the contract agree to meet the next day to assess responsibility, reimburse monies advanced, and discuss how to prevent such incidents from happening in the future.

The limits you set in your family will vary with your children's ages, your family's circumstances, and the values you wish to communicate as parents. What's most important is that your children know exactly where you stand. Discuss the reasoning behind the rules. Children are much more likely to follow them if they understand why they exist in the first place. It's important to recognize that no amount of punishment, rule setting, or grounding can prevent your child from drinking or taking other drugs if he so chooses. Only your child's good sense, self-control, and emotional health can do that.

When formulating values and limits, keep in mind that research shows that children are less likely to have drinking problems in families where the following conditions occur:

- Parents are nurturing and democratic.
- Family rituals are maintained.
- Drinking is presented in morally neutral terms.
- Drinking is not viewed as an activity for its own sake.
- Drunkenness is not viewed as a humorous condition.
- Parents model moderation if they do drink.
- Family members are neither pressured to drink nor singled out for choosing not to.
- Family policies for drinking are clearly understood and agreed to by all family members.

Here are another set of factors that appear to *increase* the likelihood that children will become problem drinkers:

- Parents are substance abusers.
- Parents employ authoritarian, permissive, or inconsistent child-rearing methods.
- Parents convey mixed, conflicting messages regarding acceptable drinking practices.
- Parents and children have distant or strained relationships.
- Parents are uninvolved in child's life.
- Family rituals have broken down.
- Parent-child communication is poor.
- Child first uses alcohol or other drugs at an early age.

A synthesis of these lists suggests that the more you practice the principles of one-day-at-a-time parenting, the less likely your children are to become substance abusers themselves.

Provide Your Child with Alternatives to Using Alcohol and Other Drugs

Although they may not know it at the time, kids usually drink and take drugs for a specific reason: They're bored, lonely, afraid, inhibited; they want to relax, have fun, seek a thrill, fit in with their peers, avoid their problems, and so on. It's natural for children to want to feel better if they're down, or to want to put some excitement in their lives if they're bored.

Help your children to see that they don't have to use chemicals to change the way they feel and deal with life. There are alternative "highs" that bring far greater rewards without any of the risks. As an exercise, ask your children to come up with "chemical-free" ways to satisfy some of the feelings and desires that often lead to alcohol and other drug use. For example, how might a child who feels sad become happier? (By talking to a friend, watching a funny video, getting involved in a project.) How might a child who's bored have some fun? (By making a two-foot-tall sandwich, going to an amusement park, taking flying lessons, inviting friends over to spend the night.) While many of these options cost little or no money, others, such as lessons, admissions, and snacks for eight teenagers spending the night, do. If your family policies and finances allow you to foot the entire bill, fine. It shows your children the extent to which you'll back their drug-free interests and activities. If you wish to share the cost with your children, their financial contribution is likely to increase their commitment and pride of accomplishment. In any case, money spent to promote drug-free ways for your children to take care of themselves will be the best investment you'll ever make!

20

Keep Coming Back
Rebuilding the Family Trust Fund

"I don't think I'd be alive today," said a recovering father, "if it weren't for those three words: *Keep coming back.*"

When we first came into recovery, we trusted nobody. Needless to say, nobody trusted us. We had proven our untrustworthiness over and over again to our employers, our co-workers, our friends, our relatives, and especially to our spouse and children.

These concentric circles of mistrust radiated from our own mistrust of ourselves. On some level we knew that we were the ones telling lies, breaking promises, and abrogating responsibilities. We were the ones who were manipulative and emotionally dishonest.

By the time we came into recovery, we couldn't even trust our drug of choice. It, too, had turned on us with a vengeance.

With no trust and no hope there was only one thing we could do: *Keep coming back.* Just by showing up, and then by working our program, we found ourselves taking a few baby steps toward trust. At first all we could trust was the unconditional love and acceptance we found at Twelve Step meetings. Then we opened up to a sponsor or program friend. We revealed some of our ugly truths and discovered that this made us no less beautiful in their eyes. As we began to feel more moral and responsible, we learned to place more trust in ourselves. And if we weren't that bad, perhaps neither was the rest of the world.

The issue of trust is a critical one if we are to rebuild family unity. Now that we are in recovery, we want to reenter our children's lives. We want to right the wrongs and make up for lost years. We want to give our children the guidance and security we failed to provide before. We want them to trust us. But why should they? Why should they consign their independence over to our authority? Why should they let down their guard and risk being hurt again?

They shouldn't. And they won't. They may, in fact, resist our efforts to come back into their lives. They are as wary of trust as we are. We cannot *make* our children trust us. All we can do is make ourselves trustworthy.

The first step in restoring trust is to recognize that trust is *behavior*. There is no basis for saying that trust exists or does not exist except as it can be seen in action. The child's trust is built up, or destroyed, as the result of what his parents do, say, emote, and demand. Eventually a "trust fund" or "mistrust fund" is endowed. This fund takes on a self-prophetic life of its own. The child who believes in his parents' trustworthiness will look for their goodness and will brush off the occasional hurtful remark or forgotten promise. The child with a basic sense of mistrust, however, will look to confirm it. He will not be affected by sporadic upswings in parental honesty, caring, and commitment.

Thus, rebuilding trust is an uphill battle. Children who have lost trust in their parents *expect* to be let down. If not today, then tomorrow; if not this week, certainly next week. Years of mistrust cannot be erased in a few weeks or months. If, however, you keep coming back, if each day, one day at a time, you show your children you can be trusted, your "trust fund" will begin to pay dividends.

How to Rebuild Trust
Love Your Child Unconditionally

If you have any doubts about the power of unconditional love, think of the role it played in your recovery. Imagine if every time you had said something pompous or self-pitying, the members of your group had withdrawn their love. How would you have felt if, upon revealing your innermost doubts and fears, your sponsor or program friends had turned away? You would have quickly lost trust in their motives and sincerity.

Love is not something you turn on and off like a faucet. Many parents, however, use withdrawal of love as their primary means of discipline and control. Usually, parents do this by becoming cold and rejecting when their child does something of which they disapprove. Sometimes the withdrawal of love is explicit: "Mommy won't love you if you're not a good boy."

Your child's trust depends on his faith that your love will always be there for him. When his actions or attitudes displease you, he must know that "Mommy loves me; she just doesn't love what I did."

Tell your children you love them. They may not know it. Make every day Valentine's Day. With younger children, slip an "I love you" note into their lunch box. With older children, give them a big hug and say the words. Your kids may feel embarrassed; they may stand in your arms like petrified trees; but they'll appreciate it. And when they mess up—when they dent the car and drop the china—let them know you love them just the same. (Although you're pretty ticked off at their carelessness!)

Just Show Up

Much of our child's mistrust of us was the result of our unreliability. We promised to come to the game—and never showed up. We promised we'd be home in time for their birthday party—and never showed up. Even when our bodies were present, our minds often were not.

You can begin to regain trust by just showing up in your children's lives. Be there at breakfast, bright-eyed and bushy-tailed. (Oh, all right—just being there is enough for now.) Be there to make their lunch and see them out the door. Be there, sober and straight, for their plays, games, concerts, and school conferences. Pick them up on time. Take them shopping or to the movies as you promised. Be there at the dinner table. Be there to help with homework and tuck them in. Trusting relationships are built out of little routines.

Listen to Your Child without Judgment or Criticism

One way children express their trust is by sharing their thoughts and feelings. Each time they do so they take a risk; they make themselves vulnerable to rejection and attack. Provide a safe haven for your children's exposures of self. Treat their ideas and emotions as you would gifts; even if they are not to your taste or liking, you can appreciate the fact that they were given.

Be Consistent

When we were using, the only consistent thing about us was our inconsistency. Our family life was in perpetual chaos and crisis. Our kids rarely knew what mood or state we'd be in. All they knew was that one way or another, we'd rock the family boat.

At this point in recovery, we need to steady the boat for our kids. We need to strive for consistency in our child-rearing practices. This doesn't mean becoming a "Roboparent" who dispenses "Yeses," "Nos," and "We'll sees" with machinelike precision. Rather, it means providing your children with the security of predictability. A recovering father offered a good example of this.

"When I was still using, I'd forget to give my kids their allowance. So they were always coming to me for money. Sometimes, when I felt particularly guilty or flush, I'd hand out ten-dollar bills. Other times, I'd bite their heads off for being spoiled and lazy, and I'd lecture them about money not growing on trees. When they protested that I hadn't given them their allowance, I'd say, 'Don't lie to me.' Things would get pretty wild and then my wife would get involved and the kids would be in tears. Now my kids get their allowance every Friday like clockwork. They know that if they need more money, they probably won't get it unless it's for an emergency or some totally unexpected expense. They also know there's a list on the refrigerator of jobs they can do to earn extra money."

This example shows how the harmful chaos of simple family routines can be tamed by consistency. Consistency, however, must be benevolent and flexible; it is there to serve, not rule. It serves by establishing a framework of expectations: in this case *when, how much, what for.* One of these expectations is that the rules are flexible. Exceptions are sometimes made. If these exceptions are made in a consistent manner, it enhances the security kids feel. In fact, the kids in this family could probably tell you exactly what they would get extra money for (a school field trip, a pair of eyeglasses that broke during gym) and what they would not get it for (an emergency ice-cream sundae, a paperback left out in the rain).

Do not impose consistency from above in the form of lists, rules, and requirements. Your children will resist such a sudden imposition of authority and structure. Rather, focus first on being consistent yourself. Examine the limits you set for your children, the expectations you hold, the reactions you have. Scrape away your fears, projections, and hidden agendas. Let go of ego and the need to control.

Consider your children's ages and levels of responsibility. Look at issues from their point of view as well as your own. You will end up with a set of values, beliefs, and feelings that should form the basis for your consistency.

When your ability to be consistent is dependent upon the participation and agreement of your children, invite their input (e.g., consistently having dinner ready at 6:00 P.M. is of little value if it conflicts with your children's after-school activities). Involve your kids in establishing family routines and expectations. Decide with them the most reasonable policies for mealtimes, curfews, bedtimes, comings and goings, phone use, car use, allowances, and so on.

Apologize

Being trustworthy doesn't mean being perfect. When you make a mistake, forget a commitment, or injure your child's trust in you, repair the damage. Apologize. Make an amend. Take an action that shows your child you regret what happened and will try to see that it doesn't happen again.

Be Honest

Honesty is always one of the first casualties in a substance-abusing family. Being true to yourself and true to your family is critical to rebuilding trust. Such honesty comes in two forms: practical honesty and emotional honesty.

Practical honesty is *telling the truth*. Alcoholics are so used to telling lies that such lies pop out almost without their knowing. Break the habit. Answer your kids' questions directly. Give reasons. Provide explanations. Your kids will value a truthful statement: "I forgot" over an untruthful one: "I couldn't get away from work."

Emotional honesty is *living the truth*. It is knowing who you are, being who you are, and expressing who you are. It is letting others do the same. When we were using, we couldn't do this. We hid our feelings; we created whatever reality suited our purposes at the time. We were empty. Because there was no "there" there, our kids had nothing to trust. Our own emotions were not the only ones we disallowed. We also disallowed those of our children. When our children were emotionally honest, they were attacked, lectured, and ridiculed. They learned never to trust us with their feelings. And, sadly, they learned to be mistrustful of themselves.

The first step in emotional honesty is to recognize one's own feelings—what's happening inside. For most addicts, learning to do this means working against the grain of a lifetime. Many of us closed down our emotional factories when we were kids. We discovered that we were safest when we hid or disavowed our feelings.

Ask an alcoholic a "how do you feel" question and chances are she'll give a "what I think" answer. For example:

Q: "How do you feel about being fired?"
A: "I feel like my boss is trying to make me the scapegoat for the company's problems."

That's a thought, not a feeling. A feeling would be: *I feel furious. I feel humiliated. I'm very depressed.*

Being able to trust yourself means being able to recognize how you feel: happy, sad, hurt, embarrassed, afraid, rejected, and so on. If it takes more than one word to describe your emotions, chances are you're looking in your head rather than in your heart. Stay in your feelings. Stop the static in your mind. Take some deep breaths. Forget about what you "should" feel, what you want to feel, what you were told to feel. Just feel.

One reason this is so hard to do is because we're conditioned to believe that there are "good" feelings (e.g., joy, love, cheerfulness, confidence) and "bad" feelings (e.g., jealousy, resentment, insecurity, helplessness). Of course some feelings make us feel good and others make us feel bad, but we are not good or bad because of them. Feelings are not inherently good or bad. They just are. A "bad" feeling may be a wonderful motivator toward growth or doing something good for others. A "good" feeling may cause us to become complacent or selfish. So which is the "good" feeling now?

We have to stop trying our feelings in the court of moral judgment. We have to stop labeling them as right, wrong, stupid, silly. What counts is not what we feel but what we do with our feelings. Do we ignore them until they infect our serenity? Do we let them poison our relationships? Do we act on them to the detriment of others? Or do we use them to solve problems, build trust, and grow?

Trusting Our Children

We all want to trust our children. But what does that mean? Trust them to do what?

- To be responsible. (According to whose standards?)
- To be careful. (Based on whose perception of risk?)
- To exercise good judgment. (According to whose principles?)

- To do what we say. (Even when we're being unreasonable?)
- To obey the law. (Even if the law is immoral?)
- To do the right thing. (In whose eyes?)
- To do the moral thing. (Based on whose values?)

You can see that the trust we extend or deny to our children is often built upon our own subjective judgments. In many cases, there are no absolute standards for what constitutes responsibility, good judgment, obedience, caution, or moral behavior. Standards vary with the particular situation, the individuals involved, the information available at the time, the context in which an event is happening. Now, I don't bring this up to suggest that children should not be held accountable for their actions because one could have a philosophical debate about moral relativism. Rather I bring it up to suggest that we often leap to the "trust issue" when what's really going on is a legitimate difference of opinion, priority, or perception. Sure, trust can be broken by willful wrongdoing: lying, cheating, stealing, carelessness. But trust can also be jeopardized unintentionally as the result of confusion, misassumptions, misunderstanding, poor communication.

When our children take an action or make a decision we don't like, before we decide that they "can't be trusted," we need to find out why they did what they did. What was going through their head? What were their assumptions and judgments? What were ours?

A recovering mother described a situation that provides an example of this: "My fourteen-year-old daughter was baby-sitting her two younger brothers one afternoon. Both boys had colds and I made it clear that they weren't to be allowed outside. I got home from work and found the apartment empty. There was a note from my daughter that said *We're at Megan's*. Megan is her best friend. I can't tell you how furious I was. I called her at Megan's and tore her ear off. 'You get home this instant. I'm never going to trust you again. You're grounded.'

"Finally, I let my daughter get a word in edgewise. It turned out that Megan had telephoned her, hysterical, saying she had fallen through a sliding glass door. So my daughter called 911, bundled up the boys, and raced over to help her friend.

"After I learned the facts, I realized that instead of trusting my daughter less, I trusted her more. Did she disobey me? Yes. But she had had a tough judgment call to make. In fact, in taking the boys with her and leaving me a note, she had used excellent judgment."

While this is a rather dramatic example, it makes it clear that we shouldn't jump to conclusions about our children's behavior without knowing the facts. We should respond to our children's intentions as much as (and in some cases more than) we do to their actions.

Good communication is essential to maintaining trust. Talk to your kids. Get things clear. Verify your assumptions. When in doubt, check it out.

21

Asking for Help
Connecting Our Children and Ourselves to the Human Lifeline

Imagine this:

> *A man has been wandering lost in the desert for a week. Starving and nearly dead from thirst, he staggers to the edge of an oasis. It is a miracle. Beyond the walls the man sees fulfillment of all his dreams: banquet tables laden with food, pools and waterfalls, cool shade, medical attention, a comfortable bed. At the front gate is a reception desk with a bell and a sign: RING FOR ASSISTANCE. The man looks at the sign. He poises his hand above the bell, then drops it to his side. He shakes his head, turns, and wanders back into the desert.*

Is the man crazy? No. Just alcoholic. And, like most alcoholics, he hates to ask anyone for assistance. There are many possible explanations for this aversion to asking for help:

- We don't recognize that we need help. Denial is our middle name.
- We were raised in an alcoholic or dysfunctional family and learned to keep our needs to ourselves.
- We fear having our request turned down or ridiculed.

- We think we're special, that nobody could possibly understand our unique feelings, needs, and sensitivities.
- We don't trust others.
- We don't know what to ask.
- We don't want to feel obligated.
- We're habituated to isolation and asking for help means making contact.

You can see from this list the extent to which our aversion to asking for help may be fueled by childhood experiences and character defects. In fact, these forces are so strong that we resist asking for help even after we have seen it bring us the miracle of recovery. How often do we come to meetings in desperate need and leave without sharing our pain with anyone? We sit silently, thinking: *They wouldn't understand; they'll think less of me; I don't want them to know I can't manage.*

One-day-at-a-time parents recognize the importance of asking for help. They know that asking for help

1. Strengthens their personal recovery,
2. Presents their children with a healthy model,
3. Generates the support and knowledge required to meet the emotional and practical challenges of parenting.

When we ask for help, we do away with false pride. We reject arrogance in favor of humility. We emerge from isolation and open ourselves to growth. Asking for help also provides others with the opportunity to give. This cycle—giving and receiving, receiving and giving—is the life force of recovery. When we fail to ask for help, it is not only our loss but the loss of those around us who would like to give of themselves.

All parents feel confused, frustrated, and inadequate at one time or another. Children do not come with instruction books. Parents are not equipped with magic wands. Child raising is hard. Growing up is hard. You—and your child—deserve all the help you can get. Here are some ways to ask for it.

Talk to Other Parents

Instead of sitting around thinking that your problems and feelings are unique, reach out. You'll discover that other parents love to talk about their children and, having been there before, can offer valuable advice and support.

Take a Parenting Workshop

If you wanted to improve your golf swing or your French, you'd take lessons. Why is it, then, that so many parents resist the idea of taking a parenting course to become better parents? Perhaps because they think it is an admission of failure. Nonsense. It is an admission of intelligence and commitment.

While parenting is not and never will be an exact science, numerous studies have shown that parenting courses can have lasting benefits for both parents and children in terms of reducing conflict, improving communication, and increasing parental confidence and consistency.

There are many ways to find such courses. Contact your child's school. Principals, guidance counselors, and Parent-Teacher Associations often know where parenting classes are offered. Contact departments of education or psychology at local colleges and universities. Many of them have research institutes that study family issues and parent-child relationships and would certainly know of parenting courses in your area. You might also try looking in the weekly events listings in local newspapers, calling area social agencies, or contacting your church or synagogue. Many cities have thriving "open universities" that offer parenting classes. (And if such courses are not available, you can always take hang gliding or wok cooking!)

Join a Twelve Step Program or Other Support Group

If you are already a member of a Twelve Step program, you know the invaluable support it provides in breaking the barriers of isolation that interfere with recovery. You may wish to explore other programs that offer help for parents, single parents, parents with chemically dependent children, codependents, victims of abuse, and so on. The experience, strength, and hope of others can help you to maintain a balanced perspective, build a network of support, and deal with the problems you are experiencing.

Seek Help from Your Child's Teachers and School Counselors

Good teachers and counselors welcome constructive parental involvement. They appreciate being told about factors at home that may affect your child's behavior at school and are often aware of factors at school that may affect your child's behavior at home. When you talk to your child's teachers, be sure to do so in a manner that respects your child's privacy and the teacher's professionalism. With their "database" of hundreds of kids and families, teachers are likely to have encountered similar problems before and often have excellent ideas for dealing with them. If you feel that the teacher *is* the problem, make an appointment to see your child's counselor or school principal.

Get Counseling

As a parent in recovery, you may be facing "problem overload." Sobriety has brought you face-to-face with long-repressed issues. You may be going through an identity crisis.

You may be dealing with social, sexual, and emotional issues you managed to avoid through years of drinking and drugging. Your marriage or primary relationship may be on the rocks. Your children's pain may be beyond your ability to ease, their behavior beyond your ability to "control."

Some problems are too much to handle by yourself. They will not go away if left unattended. They will only get worse. For problems such as these, seek professional help: Talk to a psychologist, get couples counseling, enter into family therapy. Twelve Step programs and other support groups have their limits; they were never intended to solve all personal problems, particularly those unrelated to the primary purpose of the group. Sometimes your Higher Power needs to work in tandem with a professional to achieve miracles.

Get Medical Help

People in recovery have a well-founded fear of doctors' "cures." We have all heard tales of addicts being told: "Here, you just need to relax. Have a Valium." We didn't work to get off one painkiller just to have a new one prescribed. But let's not throw the baby out with the Budweiser.

Recovering addicts may have physical or emotional problems that are endogenous; that is, originating from within the body: depression, anxiety, hypertension, chronic fatigue, attention deficit disorder, insomnia, and so on. While some of these conditions may be addressed via meditation, exercise, and/or diet, others may require medication. In fact, many of us used alcohol and other drugs as self-medication for depression, anxiety, sleeping disorders, and other problems.

In a pamphlet entitled *The A.A. Member—Medications and Other Drugs,* the official position of Alcoholics Anonymous on the use of psychoactive drugs is stated as follows:

> *. . . It becomes clear that just as it is wrong to enable or support any alcoholic to become readdicted to any drug, it's equally wrong to deprive any alcoholic of medication which*

can alleviate or control other disabling physical and/or emotional problems.[15]

The decision to take medication for depression or anxiety is a difficult and personal one. The recovering parent considering such a step should ask herself a number of questions:

- Are the fears and blues I feel a normal and expected part of recovery?
- Am I overreacting to the ups and downs of life?
- Am I seeking an unrealistic level of serenity?
- Am I being impatient about my progress?
- Am I working my program? Do I exercise, meditate, pray, and practice healthy eating and sleeping habits?
- Are there external causes for the way I feel that will either pass with time or respond to actions taken (e.g., problems at work, marital troubles, financial insecurity, family crises)?

If, upon considering these questions, you conclude that you are doing everything possible to combat your anxiety or depression "naturally" and still are unable to function on a day-to-day basis, then you may need to take psychoactive drugs and/or other medications.

Many safe, legal, nonaddictive drugs exist today to combat depression, anxiety, sleeping disorders, and so on. It is essential that you tell any physician treating you that you are in recovery so that medications that pose a high risk of abuse and readdiction can be avoided.

Your body's chemistry, the same chemistry that predisposed you to addiction, is still "out to get you" in recovery. Fight it with everything you have—including medical attention and safe prescription drugs.

Ask for Help from Friends, Sponsors, and Fellow Twelve Step Members

"Keeping a stiff upper lip" makes about as much sense as "keeping a drunk dry." There's no reason to suffer needlessly. If recovery has taught us anything, it is that much of our pain is due to disconnecting from the human race. Invariably we feel better when we speak at a meeting or confide in our friends. In fact, close, supportive friendships have been associated with lower mortality rates,[16] lower incidence of heart disease,[17] and fewer complications in pregnancy for women undergoing stressful events.[18] One study found that women without a close friend were ten times more likely to be depressed than were women with a close friend.[19]

When life's problems get you down, when troubles erupt in your family or with your children, talk to your friends, your sponsor, your fellow Twelve Step members. They may be able to offer sound advice or to share something helpful from their own experience. Their love and support will make you feel less alone with your problem and better equipped to solve it.

Ask Your Higher Power for Help

With all "his" children, your Higher Power is bound to know something about parenting! Tap into God's wisdom and guidance. Use the strength and spiritual calm your Higher Power gives you to be patient and accepting, to love unconditionally, to let go and let God. Pray to your Higher Power for your child and family. Pray for serenity. Pray for courage. Pray for wisdom.

Ask Your Kids for Help

We often assume that we should hide our problems from our children. We tell ourselves that we don't want to worry or burden them. We don't want to admit that we're in a real pickle or that we've messed up. We don't want them to know that we haven't got all the answers. Granted, there are some problems and circumstances that would best be kept to ourselves. This doesn't mean, however, that we should act as if nothing is wrong. Children are too smart and too sensitive to be taken in by a plastic smile. We owe them more than such dishonesty. Let your kids know when you're in a bind. You don't have to tell them all the details. But the truth, even if it is unpleasant, will cause them less harm than their own fearful imaginings.

There's another reason for telling your kids when you have a problem: Children can be a big help. They are a highly empathic species and usually rise to the occasion when someone respects them enough to ask for their assistance. This assistance may be of a practical nature: extra baby-sitting, cooking, or cleaning. Children also understand what it means to be going through a hard time. If you are hurting, ask your children for their support and forbearance. Let them know that you don't mean to be short-tempered or distracted; if appropriate, share with them the source of your anxiety.

Finally, when problems include your children, ask for their help in solving them. Children would much rather participate in the process than have solutions handed down from above. Besides, kids often see the situation from a different perspective. Their input is necessary if a lasting solution is to be found.

Helping Our Children to Ask for Help

Your children, having grown up in a family with a substance abuse problem, may themselves be reluctant to ask for help. In the past, their requests may have triggered lectures and arguments or been ignored, forgotten, or belittled. They may have learned to keep their needs and questions hidden. If so, there are several things you can do to help them overcome their reluctance to ask you and others for advice and support.

Make an Explicit Amend

Acknowledge to your children that you were not always there to help them in the past. In your own words, made appropriate to the age of your child, you can say: "I know that there have been times when you've asked for my help and I couldn't or didn't give it. I'm sorry that that happened and I wish things had been different. I can't change the past, but I can do everything in my power to see that it never happens again. There are times when we all need help from others. I want you to know that I would like to help you whenever I can. If you ask for my help, you will be giving me not a burden but a gift."

Respect Your Child's Request

You know how reluctant *you* can be when it comes to asking for help. It makes you feel vulnerable; it exposes you to possible rejection, judgment, or criticism. Use this knowledge to respond to your child's requests:

- Don't ridicule your child when he asks for your help.
- Don't turn requests for help into lecture opportunities.
- Don't dismiss your child's request with a curt remark such as: "I'm busy" or "Can't you do it yourself?"

If you are busy and can't help, say so. But say it in a way that reinforces your child's willingness to seek help in the future: "I'm so glad you came to me. I would love to help you. But I can't do it right now because I have to get this finished. I'll have some time later this afternoon. How about then?"

Whether it's a four-year-old with a knot in his shoelace, a seven-year-old with a flat tire, or a sixteen-year-old with an algebra problem, they all want the same thing—you. They are placing something very precious in your hands—their trust. Handle it with care.

It is also important to realize that when your child requests your help, she may be asking for something else: attention, structure, solace. For example: Your child asks for help with her homework. You know she can easily do the work by herself. If you say: "I know you know how to do it, and I'm not going to do your work for you," you've slammed the door in her face. By responding to the *words* of the request, you have missed the emotional need underlying it—a booster shot of love, a desire for companionship, an escape from boredom. When you respond to your child's *need,* you open doors: "Why don't we work together in the study. I have some 'homework' too. And if either of us gets stuck, we can ask the other. Okay?"

Unnecessary requests for help may also be your child's way of testing you. Are you really going to be there for her? Are you going to break your promises? Recognize these requests for what they are. Let your child test you. She has every reason to be suspicious. As you show that you are there, this type of request should diminish and eventually disappear.

Keep in mind that your child's asking for help may also be a form of insurance against being chastised for doing something wrong. Many children of alcoholics have seen their tiniest error trigger a severe punishment, a family fight, or a drinking binge. The fear these children feel causes them to narrow their world to reduce exposure. Now that you are in recovery, your child's requests for help may be a holdover, a protective mechanism: "After all," your child reasons, "if Dad helps, how can he blame me if something goes wrong?"

Your best response to your child's understandable fear is to show that you don't blame her when things go wrong. Don't lecture, yell, hit, or shame. Instead, help her to learn from her mistakes, to right the wrong or undo the damage, to recognize that trying and failing is better than never having tried in the first place.

Encourage Your Child to Find Her Own Sources of Help

You can't solve all your child's problems. Nor should you. In some cases, you may even be your child's problem. "Being there" means knowing when not to be there, knowing when your child needs to seek help outside the family.

Encourage your child to speak to teachers, school counselors, coaches, clergy, and friends. Let her know that you understand her need to keep certain feelings and problems to herself. Let her know that you will not be threatened if she wants to see a therapist. Let her know that support groups exist to help people with feelings and issues similar to hers. If she is receptive, help her to find them. If she is resistant, time and the benefits she sees you enjoying may change her mind.

When you come to your children for assistance, when you and your kids talk to a family therapist, when you stop at a gas station and ask for directions, you show your children that asking for help is something you value and act upon in your own life. You present your children with a model of humility and responsibility. You show that you are willing to join hands with others in order to learn and to grow.

22

Keep It Simple
Setting Parenting Priorities

"When I was still drugging," said a recently divorced father of three, "I used to go out to this very beautiful lake to get wasted. I thought that if I could just be by myself and 'think,' I could solve all my problems. So I'd start thinking about how much I hated my job, and how I didn't have any money, and how my wife was threatening to leave me, and how my kid was getting into trouble at school, and what I really needed to do was change jobs, make a million bucks, and put my wife and kid into therapy. But I couldn't look for a new job without a resume, and I couldn't put together a resume because I didn't have a computer, and I couldn't get a computer because I didn't have any money, and if I didn't have any money, I couldn't afford therapy—so there was no way I'd ever change jobs or straighten things out at home. It felt like I was trapped inside a giant ball of string, and the more I tried to untangle it, the more tangled it became. I swear, two minutes of thinking was the most exhausting thing I could do!"

"I still feel that way a lot of the time," commented a recovering mother who was listening to our conversation. "It seems as if everything in my life needs fixing but I don't know where to begin. So I end up doing nothing."

Alcoholics have an absolute gift for complicating the simple and obscuring the obvious. If the road is straight, we'll find a detour. If the path is clear, we'll dig potholes. Too bad they don't give Nobel prizes for obfuscation!

Nowhere is *Keeping it simple* more essential than in raising our children. One-day-at-a-time parents recognize how much needless worry and trouble they create for themselves and their kids when they lose sight of what is important. Several recovering parents spoke about this. One father shared the following experience:

"My kids had been bugging me to build them a treehouse in the backyard. So I'd promise we'd do it Saturday, and then Saturday would come and I'd go off and get drunk, so I'd promise we'd do it *next* Saturday and, well, you know how that goes. Eventually they stopped asking. Anyway, one of the first things I wanted to do in recovery was build that treehouse. I got my kids all revved up about it and took out a big pad of paper and started to plan and draw and make lists of everything we would need. This wasn't going to be just a treehouse. This was going to be the greatest learning experience two kids had ever had. I'd teach them about tools and oak trees and dimension lumber; pulleys, levers, screws, Euclidean geometry—you name it. This was going to make up for lost years and cement our relationship for life. The kids were getting more and more squirmy until, finally, one of them said, 'Can't we just build it?'

"For a minute, I felt hurt and rejected and then I remembered: *Keep it simple, stupid!* All they'd ever wanted was a board or two nailed into the tree. Well, an hour later they had their boards and a couple of steps and ropes, and you'd have thought I'd built the Taj Mahal the way they were beaming. That was probably the greatest learning experience I ever had."

"I can relate to that," laughed a mother. "All it takes is for my daughter to ask me how much two and two is and I'm organizing her notebook and teaching multiplication tables."

It's parent nature to want to manage and improve all areas of a child's life. It's addict nature to want to do it overnight. Put the two together and you've got an impossible, no-win situation for both parent and child.

One-day-at-a-time parents do not get paralyzed by the enormity of everything. They prioritize. They set goals. They break tasks into manageable pieces. They avoid hassles and conflicts by eliminating, wherever possible, the conditions that breed them. Instead of yelling, "Don't touch!" they place valuable objects out of reach. Instead of getting angry when their child throws a whole plate of food on the floor, they set out only a few mouthfuls at a time. Instead of saying, "Go play but don't get your clothes dirty," they dress their child in old clothes.

You may look at your family and feel overwhelmed by things that need "fixing." How do you deal with them all? You don't. You only deal with the things that are important. That keeps it simple. Not easy. Just simple.

For example: It's a weekend afternoon. You've wasted the whole day staring at your list of Things to Do: clean house, wash car, go through receipts for taxes, pick Ned up at Little League, and so on. You're feeling antsy, fearful, and depressed. What do you do? You go to a meeting. Why? Because you know what's important: (1) staying clean and sober, (2) fulfilling your parental responsibilities, and (3) rebuilding healthy roles and relationships within your family.

When priorities are clear, everything falls into place. So, to stay clean and sober, you go to the five o'clock meeting; to fulfill your parental responsibilities, you pick Ned up at Little League and take the kids shopping for the things they need. Later that night, you work on the taxes. And, no, the house doesn't get cleaned, the car doesn't get washed, and the shirts don't get ironed. But guess what? It doesn't matter! Because you had a good day. You were there for your kids and you didn't pick up a drink or a drug.

Keeping it simple is a lens you look through when setting goals and prioritizing actions. First, gaze at the broadest landscape. Once your goals are established at that level, zoom in on smaller areas within the frame. Set new goals and priorities. Each time you narrow your focus, say: "Okay, at this scale, for *this* goal, what is most important?" This way you avoid the paralysis that comes from feeling overwhelmed. You break infinity into baby steps.

For recovering parents, this is a wonderful and reassuring tool. Without it we would be buried by the enormity of our responsibilities. We would have no antidote to the compulsive and controlling nature of our personalities. We would have no way of dealing with our problems or the problems of our children.

One recovering father was having a particularly hard time with his fourteen-year-old son. "The kid's driving me crazy," he said.

"You mean you're letting your kid drive you crazy," I replied.

"What do you mean?"

Suspecting that this was not the best moment to launch into my lecture about stinkin' thinkin' and Rational-Emotive Therapy, I said, "Tell me what he does that drives you crazy." Without further prompting, this father let loose with a list a mile long of "Things about My Kid that Annoy Me":

Messy room.

Earring.

Plays music too loud.

Ties up phone.

Borrows tools and doesn't put them back.

Leaves the refrigerator door open.

Wears sneakers untied.

Purposely rips brand-new jeans.

Doesn't rewind videotapes.

Talks with his mouth full.

Loses belongings.

Takes too many showers.

Just as I was catching my breath, the father began a new list of "Things My Kid Needs to Get His Act Together About":

Controlling his temper.

Lying.

Failing math and French.

Making friends.

Getting along better with his mother.

Being more organized.

Said list was soon followed by "My Child's Problems":

Seems sad and lonely.

Gets teased at school.

Says teachers don't like him.

Thinks he's dumb.

Wants and doesn't have a girlfriend.

This deluge of parental frustration finally concluded with "Problems between My Child and Me":

We barely talk to each other.

Unspoken anger and resentments.

Power struggles over limits.

Every conversation ends in argument.

The minutia and magnitude of this father's concerns left *me* breathless and exhausted—and it wasn't even my kid!

"Look," I said to the father. "You're trying to do everything. You have to keep it simple. Forget the sneakers. Forget the showers, the refrigerator door, the earring, the tools, the videotapes. Forget about fixing his relationship with his mother. You can't do that. It's not that some of these things don't matter. It's just that they aren't the priorities."

So what does a parent do when he feels overwhelmed by concerns and responsibilities and "things to fix"? First, make a list. Get it all down on paper. Then, as you read down your list, ask yourself

- Am I trying to control people, places, and things I have no business or power to control?
- Will this item matter in an hour, a week, or a year from now?
- What's the worst thing that could happen if I do nothing?
- Would a change in my attitude eliminate the problem?
- Can I turn it over to my Higher Power?
- Can I settle for progress instead of perfection?
- Are irrational shoulds, musts, and awfuls fueling my frenzy?

With these questions in mind, let's go back and reread the father's list from the preceding pages. Do the items appear different in the light of this *Keep it simple* perspective? They do to me.

Messy room. (So don't go in it.)

Earring. (Oh, puh-lease. It's his ear.)

Plays music too loud. (You mean, too loud for *you.* Don't complain. Solve the problem. Headphones? Quiet hours? Soundproofing? Change the location of his room?)

Ties up phone. (Define the problem more clearly. Are important calls not getting through? Are siblings fighting? Are message units adding up? Is this the *phones-shouldn't-be-in-constant-use* "should"? Where is such a rule written? Have you considered putting in a second line? Getting call waiting? Establishing use policies? Be glad he's home using the phone and not out getting into trouble.)

Borrows tools and doesn't put them back. (It's wonderful he's got so many projects going that need tools! Explain that you're pleased he uses them but that you would like to be able to find them easily when you need them. What does *he* suggest?)

Leaves the refrigerator door open. (So do you. Next item.)

Purposely rips brand-new jeans. (And you used to purposely tie-dye brand-new T-shirts.)

Doesn't rewind videotapes. (Annoying but not worthy of a battle.)

Talks with his mouth full. (It's great he's communicating. And one day a girlfriend will cure him of the habit with one comment.)

Loses belongings. (He'll have to go without or replace them himself.)

Takes too many showers. (Be thankful it's not the other way around!)

One can continue in this fashion with the entire list. When you cross off the items that just aren't a big deal, the items that aren't any of the father's business, the items that can easily be solved at a family meeting, the items whose consequences properly devolve upon the son, the items that result from unrealistic expectations, three remain:

Seems sad and lonely.
Thinks he's dumb.
Unspoken anger and resentments.

Aren't these the three issues that *really* matter? The ones with the most far-reaching consequences for this child's life? *Keeping it simple* has brought clarity and focus to the situation. This doesn't necessarily mean that these issues will be easy to address. It will certainly be easier, however, to address three major priorities than to flail about among forty.

The child in this example has little self-esteem and is hurting emotionally. He could be encouraged to attend a Twelve Step group for children of chemically dependent parents and to see a therapist. The father could talk to his son's teachers to learn more about why his son "thinks he's dumb." The father could support his son's interests and areas of strength outside of school. He could relate to his child through the principles of the program, doing his utmost to make amends, to stop taking his son's inventory, to focus on the good, to communicate love and acceptance, to work to create a nonjudgmental atmosphere that allows for the expression of his son's long-pent-up hurt and anger. Doesn't this seem a lot more important than whether a kid's jeans are ripped?

Helping Children to Keep It Simple

Kids, too, can feel overwhelmed by increasing social, emotional, and academic pressures in their lives. There are a number of things your child can do to keep things simple.

Prioritize

We often act as if children somehow automatically learn how to organize their lives. Well, most of us never learned how to do these things—why would our kids? If your child complains, "I have too much to do," if he appears stressed and unhappy, if he inhabits some distant planet except for brief pit stops at the dinner table, suggest that he make a list of everything on his docket. By putting things down in black and white he can turn a vague, vast cloud of anxiety into a discrete (albeit lengthy) statement of competing obligations. Once his list is finished, help him to set goals and prioritize by asking him:

"Which things do you *have* to do?"

"Out of the things you have to do, which are most important?"

"Which things would you *like* to do?"

"Which things could you let slide?"

"What needs to be done *today?*"

Explain to your child that this type of analysis forms a basis for making decisions and taking action. The approach can also be used to deal with personal problems and emotional upheaval if he asks himself:

"Which things are bothering me the most?"

"Which of these can I do something about?"

"What can I do today?"

Break Tasks Down into Manageable Steps

Even a single goal can be overwhelming. Young children who are told, "Go clean up your room," often stare at the said room in a state of confused "where-to-begin" paralysis.

You can help your child if you show him how to break a task down into smaller components:

"I'd like you to go put all your toys in the toy bin."

"Okay, now put all your animal friends on the bed."

"Next, take any clothes on the floor and put them in the hamper in the laundry room."

This process can also be explained to older children. For example, your child might, after making a list, decide that her greatest priorities are to improve her grade in science, patch up a friendship, and write a paper for history. Help her to break these large goals into smaller chunks. She could plan to tackle the history paper in the following manner:

Monday I'll go to the library and check out the materials I need. Tuesday I'll read them and take notes. Wednesday I'll make an outline, and so forth.

When you *Keep it simple,* you ask yourself every day: What can I do *today* to make progress toward the goals I have set? When you *Keep it simple,* your priorities as a parent become clear:

Know your child.

Enjoy your child.

Empathize with your child.

Practice honesty and humility in your relations with your child.

Identify and solve problems as they come up.

Trust in your Higher Power to help.

Speak to your child with respect.

Include your child in decision making.

Model the attitudes and values you believe in.

Provide for your child's physical, practical, social, emotional, and educational needs.

Love and accept your child without condition.

Encourage your child's interests and creativity.

And stay clean and sober!

23

It Gets Better
Keeping Track of Our Progress
as Parents and as a Family

Rarely have we seen a parent fail
who has thoroughly followed our path.[20]

As you apply the tools of recovery to raising your children and healing your family, you will want to monitor whether you are, indeed, following the "path." The daily inventories presented in this chapter are designed to help you do so. The Daily Family Inventory assesses your progress toward healthy family functioning. Personalize it by listing the specific goals and problems upon which your family is focusing its attention.

Daily Parenting Inventory 1 and Daily Parenting Inventory 2 assess your progress as a one-day-at-a-time parent. The first inventory is based on character strengths and weaknesses. The second describes parenting in terms of behaviors and attitudes. Many parents find the two perspectives to be complementary and take both inventories each day. Other parents prefer one form to the other.

"No one among us has been able to maintain anything like perfect adherence to these parenting principles. We are not saints. The point is, that we are willing to grow...."[21]

Daily Family Inventory

Current family goal(s)   Ongoing family problems(s)

_____   _____

_____   _____

Place a Y (Yes) or N (No) to indicate whether the statement applies
Today, as a family, we . . .

	1	2	3	4	5	6	7	8	9	10	11	12	13	14*
Made progress toward solving a family problem.														
Dealt constructively with anger or conflicts.														
Discussed ideas and issues of mutual concern.														
Communicated openly and honestly without being unkind.														
Spent time together having fun.														
Maintained appropriate roles for parents and children.														
Behaved affectionately toward one another.														
Shared responsibilities fairly.														
Accomplished basic tasks of living.														
Exchanged necessary information.														
Encouraged and accepted the expression of feelings.														
Cooperated to achieve personal and family goals.														
Lived according to our values.														
Provided for individual time and space.														
Respected and enjoyed one another's uniqueness.														
Shared a family ritual.														
_____														
_____														

Beware of NOs!   Strive for YESes!

* 1–14 in days

Daily Parenting Inventory 1

Place a - or a + in the appropriate column
to indicate which of the paired traits applies

Today, as a parent, I was . . .

-	1	2	3	4	5	6	7	8	9	10	11	12	13	14*	+
Arbitrary															Fair
Judgmental															Accepting
Rigid															Flexible
Unreliable															Dependable
Resentful															Forgiving
Grandiose															Humble
Selfish															Generous
Humorless															Cheerful
Suspicious															Trusting
Unappreciative															Grateful
Cold															Affectionate
Full of Fear															Full of Faith
Dishonest															Honest
Autocratic															Democratic
Out of Control															Self-Controlled
Manipulative															Straightforward
Inconsistent															Consistent
Critical															Supportive
Intolerant															Open-Minded
Irresponsible															Responsible
Abusive															Loving
Bad Example															Good Example

BEWARE of -   STRIVE for +

* 1–14 in days

Daily Parenting Inventory 2

Current family goal(s)

_____

_____

Ongoing family problems(s)

_____

_____

Place a Y (Yes) or N (No) to indicate whether the statement applies

Today, as a parent . . .	1	2	3	4	5	6	7	8	9	10	11	12	13	14*
I made progress toward my parenting goal(s).														
I made necessary amends and/or apologies.														
I accepted my children's feelings.														
I supported my children's goals and interests.														
I spent time with my children.														
I spoke to my children without attacking, blaming, or labeling them.														
I listened to my children without ridiculing, judging, or dismissing their thoughts and feelings.														
I trusted my children.														
I respected my children's privacy.														
I allowed my children to make their own decisions except when to do so would cause harm to them or others.														
I set consistent yet flexible limits.														
I treated my children with courtesy.														
I noticed and commented upon my children's accomplishments and good behavior.														
I expressed an interest in my children's lives.														
I looked after my children's practical and physical needs.														
I extended to myself the same tolerance, kindness, and patience I try to extend to my children.														
I told my children I loved them.														

Beware of NOs!   Strive for YESes!

Parenting One Day at a Time. ©1996 by Alex J. Packer, Ph.D. Published by Hazelden. Reproduction for individual, personal use is permissible.
* 1–14 in days

If you are willing to let go of old parenting ideas, to be fearless and thorough, you *will* grow as a parent. The tools of recovery *will* work miracles for you and your family. But it's going to take a lot of effort, faith, and perseverance to master them. Along the way to greater family health there are bound to be moments when you'll feel discouraged and frustrated. At those times, just remember, practice makes perf—er, progress.

Notes

1. Alcoholics Anonymous World Services, *Alcoholics Anonymous,* 3d ed. (New York: AA World Services, 1976), 58–59. This is a play on the famous phrase in the "How It Works" chapter of the Big Book: "Remember that we deal with alcohol—cunning, baffling, powerful!"

2. E. E. Maccoby and J. A. Martin, "Socialization in the Context of the Family: Parent-Child Interaction," in *Socialization, Personality and Social Development, vol. 4. Handbook of Child Psychology,* ed. E. M. Hetherington (New York: Wiley, 1983).

3. A. G. Billings and R. H. Moos, "Psychosocial Processes of Recovery Among Alcoholics and Their Families: Implications for Clinicians and Program Evaluators," *Addictive Behaviors* 8 (1983): 205–18.

4. Alcoholics Anonymous World Services, *Alcoholics Anonymous,* 3d ed. (New York: AA World Services, 1976), 59.

5. Albert Ellis, "Rational Emotive Therapy," *Current Psychotherapies,* 3d ed., ed. R. J. Corsini and D. Wedding (Itasca, Ill.: Peacock, 1989), 233–34.

6. Adapted from H. S. Young, "Principles of Assessment and Methods of Treatment with Adolescents: Special Considerations," in *Rational-Emotive Approaches to the Problems of Childhood,* ed. A. Ellis and M. E. Bernard (New York: Plenum Press, 1983).

7. A. Bandura, *Principles of Behavior Modification* (New York: Holt, Rinehart & Winston, 1969).

8. M. R. Yarrow and P. M. Scott, "Imitation of Nurturant and Non-nurturant Models," *Journal of Personality and Social Psychology* 23 (1972): 259–70.

9. M. R. Yarrow, P. M. Scott, and C. Z. Waxler, "Learning Concern for Others," *Developmental Psychology* 8 (1973): 240–60.

10. J. H. Bryan and N. H. Walbek, "Preaching and Practicing Generosity: Children's Actions and Reactions," *Child Development* 41 (1970): 329–53.

11. R. D. O'Connor, "Modification of Social Withdrawal Through Symbolic Modeling," *Journal of Applied Behavior Analysis* 2 (1969): 15–22.

12. M. Csapo, "Peer Models Reverse the 'One Bad Apple Spoils the Barrel' Theory," *Teaching Exceptional Children* 5 (1972): 20–24.

13. M. Shafii, R. Lavely, and R. Jaffe, "Meditation and the Prevention of Alcohol Abuse," *Alcohol Health and Research World* (summer 1976): 18–21.

14. L. A. Bennett, S. J. Wolin, and D. Reiss, "Deliberate Family Process: A Strategy for Protecting Children of Alcoholics," *British Journal of Addiction* 83 (1988): 821–29.

15. Alcoholics Anonymous World Services, *The A.A. Member—Medications and Other Drugs* (New York: AA World Services, 1984), 9.

16. L. F. Beekman and S. Syme, "Social Networks, Host Resistance, and Mortality: A Nine-Year Follow-up Study of Alameda County Residents," *American Journal of Epidemiology* 109, no. 2 (1979): 186–204.

17. S. Wolf and N. Goodell, *Behavioral Science in Clinical Medicine* (Springfield, Ill.: Charles C. Thomas, 1976), 16–19, 162–73.

18. K. B. Nuckols et al., "Psychosocial Assets, Life Crises, and the Prognosis of Pregnancy," *American Journal of Epidemiology* 95, no. 5 (1972): 331–441.

19. G. W. Brown et al., "Social Class and Psychiatric Disturbance Among Women in an Urban Population," *Sociology* 9, no. 2 (1975): 225–54.

20. Alcoholics Anonymous World Services, *Alcoholics Anonymous,* 3d ed. (New York: AA World Services, 1976), 58. This is a play on the phrase "Rarely have we seen a person fail who has thoroughly followed our path."

21. Alcoholics Anonymous World Services, *Alcoholics Anonymous,* 3d ed. (New York: AA World Services, 1976), 60. This is a play on the phrase "No one among us has been able to maintain anything like perfect adherence to these principles."

Index

About the Author

Alex J. Packer is president and CEO of FCD Educational Services, Inc. Founded in 1976, FCD (the initials stand for Freedom from Chemical Dependency) is a Boston-based nonprofit organization that provides alcohol, tobacco, and other drug education for schools and colleges in the United States and abroad.

An educator and developmental psychologist, Packer is the author of numerous books for parents and teenagers including the award-winning *Bringing Up Parents: The Teenager's Handbook, 365 Ways to Love Your Child,* and the best-selling *How Rude! The Teenagers' Guide to Good Manners, Proper Behavior, and Not Grossing People Out.*

For eight years, Packer was the headmaster of an independent middle school in Washington, D.C. He has since served as director of education for the Capital Children's Museum. A specialist in adolescence, substance abuse, family relations, and parenting, Packer holds undergraduate and master's degrees from Harvard University and a Ph.D. in educational and developmental psychology from Boston College.

Packer lectures nationwide and currently serves as chairman of the advisory board of COASA (Children of Alcoholism and Substance Abuse, Inc.), a nonprofit organization that provides services for children from homes where substance abuse has occurred.